CLASSIC DOLLS

Editor: Amy Handy
Production manager: Dana Cole
Jacket design: Julie Rauer

Library of Congress Cataloging-in-Publication Data
Tosa, Marco.
[Effetto bambola. English]
Classic dolls / by Marco Tosa :
photographs by Graziella Pellicci.
p.   cm.
Translation of: Effetto bambola.
Bibliography: p.
Includes index.
ISBN 0-89659-972-8
1. Dolls—History.   I. Pellicci, Graziella.   II. Title.
NK4894.A2T6713   1989
688.7'221—dc 19   88-31248
CIP

CLASSIC DOLLS

TEXT BY
MARCO TOSA

PHOTOGRAPHY BY
GRAZIELLA PELLICCI

ABBEVILLE PRESS · PUBLISHERS · NEW YORK

CONTENTS

PREFACE

A problem besetting any writer of a book on dolls is that anything one can write about them—and much has been written—succeeds only in limiting the scope of this endlessly fascinating subject. To understand its essential character, there is really no substitute for holding in one's hand an antique manikin or baby doll, dressed in its original outfit and painted in the colours of its period, for it alone can convey its true personality and explain its hold over the heart of the collector. Words can, however, provide valuable historical and technical information and photographic images help to determine the nature of the doll in visual terms.

Huge quantities of dolls of all kinds have been produced over the past two centuries alone, yet fine examples are increasingly hard to find because so many people are hunting for that legendary and coveted 'unique piece.' As a result, record prices are now being paid at international auctions. But chance discoveries in attics and forgotten trunks still happen, and every collector lives in hope of finding an abandoned doll and recapturing that spirit of another age that constitutes much of its magic.

It is partly the desire to recover the past, and memories of one's own past in particular, that leads one to start collecting in the first place, but there are countless other factors that contribute to the irresistible appeal of the doll: the skill and inventiveness of the great manufacturers of the golden age, the delightful and often very intricate costumes that reflected fashions and lifestyles so vividly, and above all the individuality of the dolls themselves.

The passion of the collector and the roots from which it grew are so complex and personal as to make a rich source of material for students of the human psyche. But the origin of the passion often lies in a nostalgia for an archetypal past that never really existed and that has somehow been idealized in our minds, the doll embodying all that seems now to have been romantic, innocent, and beautiful about a world that has gone forever.

One of the stories that I remember most clearly from my childhood is a tale about dolls, and perhaps the strength of the impression it made on me was an intimation of what the future would hold. I believe now that it was the first link in the chain, and that it gave me an impetus to which I responded only much later, when I began to explore an area that had already been coloured by that story and by my own imagination. Finding a doll lying broken in a plastic bag among other discarded things, I sensed the excitement and delight that an archaeologist feels at the discovery of a fragile relic of the long-distant past. That first thrill led on to a detailed study of the subject that has occupied me for many years and that I know can never be exhausted because its scope is boundless.

'A doll is animated, like every object and work of art, by the spirit of whoever looks at it.' So said a dear and wise friend of mine, and it is a phrase that I often recall and that is associated in my mind with the very earliest days of my doll collecting; it will therefore serve well to introduce my text.

I
THE EARLY YEARS

The evolutionary history of the doll has moved in step with the development of attitudes to play, a fact confirmed by the existence in earliest times of dolls now lost for ever: unimaginable dolls, made of unspecified materials, with features that may have been purely symbolic or may have faithfully imitated reality. We simply do not know; we know they existed but no trace of them has been found.

Play itself, which is essentially liberating and creative, among the first instincts of man, has always been responsible for producing its own playthings, ephermeral objects that are often invented and destroyed by the same child. Taking a wide variety of forms, the most ancient toys certainly have as their foundation and source of inspiration the world closest to the child, that of the immediate family. Seen through the eyes of a child, the doll is an image of man, an inanimate imitation to which a degree of expressiveness can be attributed and on which affection can be lavished. Even today,

such 'primary' toys dominate infancy and adolescence, and are often enjoyed in adulthood too. The doll is a model of a human being, and as such has no equal (unless it can be said to compare with the puppet); it has its own distinct and recognizable form and is always invested with a degree of humanity.

In searching for traces of dolls in the distant past, it is easy to be misled by the sacred images and votive offerings that every civilization has produced in abundance. Even religious ritual, for which such objects were intended, sometimes included some form of 'play.' There is a danger, therefore, in labelling as dolls the many figures—in terracotta, wood, clay, and all manner of other materials, seen in museums all over the world—whose original function is uncertain. Strenuous attempts have been made to define their purpose, and it is even possible that they were intended as playthings, underlining the capacity of a child to invest almost any object with the properties of a toy. In this book, however, the 'doubtful' dolls will be omitted and only those that were be-

A detail of the beautifully modelled head of the doll found in Rome in 1889 in the tomb of Crepereia during excavations for the new Palace of Justice. It has been described as 'strange, disturbing . . . in some magical way it seems to represent Crepereia herself . . . or perhaps it is an image of her future life.'

yond question created as dolls in the accepted sense will be included.

One of the earliest, now in the British Museum in London, can be dated to the middle of the fifth century BC. It is made of baked clay and came originally from Greece, and there is no doubt about its original function as a plaything. The head and torso are modelled in one piece and are anatomically accurate, and the details of the hairstyle are clearly defined. The legs and arms move by means of a fine cord threaded through pierced holes. Though 'modern' in technical construction, it shows in its design a concern for the world of the child and the attention given to play and ritual, of great importance not only in terms of their formative influence but also in social and religious spheres.

At the height of the Greek civilization dolls marked the stages of childhood and puberty, and when a young woman embarked on married life she was given a doll dedicated to the goddess Artemis, as if to bridge the gap between the period when play imitated the adult role and the moment when mimicry was replaced by reality.

Taking on a wide range of functions, the doll adapted itself to the civilization that produced it, slowly losing its significance as an object through which emotion and instinct could be expressed. In this way it moved ever closer to the adult world to which, as we shall see later on, it became closely allied.

A clay doll, probably Athenian, from the fifth century AD.

On 12 May 1889, in the Prati district of Rome, the sarcophagus of Crepereia Tryphaena was opened. Great enthusiasm and excitement greeted the event, which brought to light the remains of a young Roman woman who had lived in the second century AD. But the most fascinating aspect of the discovery was that, together with the precious jewels with which the body was buried, a doll was found. Exquisitely made, it was accompanied by a small ivory casket, a tiny key ring, earrings, two small silver mirrors, and two combs made of bone. The doll represents an example of the high level of achievement reached in this area of craftsmanship at the time, and displays the characteristics typical of an object that by then had been perfected as a plaything. Twenty-three centimetres (9 inches) high and made of ivory, it has a complex articular structure, its joints (shoulders, elbows, even knees) moving on pivots, while the torso and head are carved in one piece. Here the qualities of Greek terracotta dolls, and of earlier and contemporary Roman ones, have been brought to their highest point. The Crepereia doll is extremely skilfully made, especially in the modelling of the features and hairstyle, which was inspired by the fashion adopted by the Empresses Faustina Minore and Faustina Maggiore. Such meticulous care in reproducing detail makes it possible to date the figure to AD 150–60. A rich assort-

12

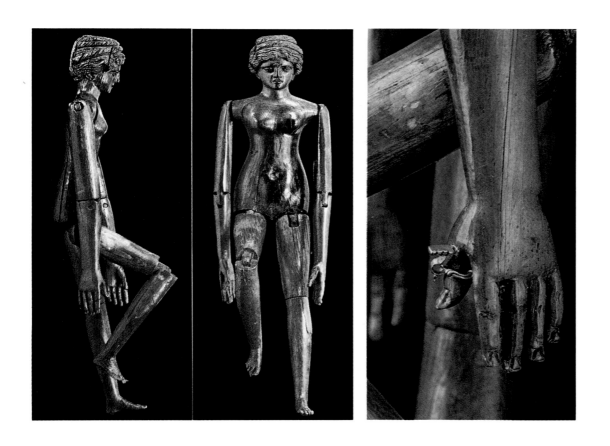

ment of jewels was found with it and, though the garments themselves have unfortunately been lost, there were traces of fossilized cloth near by.

Apart from this celebrated doll, a number of other beautifully made and valuable examples from the ancient world still exist, such as the one named after the vestal virgin Cossinia—found with gold ornaments at the neck, wrists, and ankles—and those now in the Vatican Museum. These dolls, which owe their survival to the materials of which they were made, probably shared children's attention with other poorer examples in bone—just a few centimetres high, with stiff bodies and rudimentary limbs joined by a string threaded through holes—and also with rag dolls, stuffed and stitched very simply, probably similar to those in the British Museum that have miraculously been handed down to us.

The development of the doll, which by now had a precise identity and was intended for a variety of purposes, continued alongside the story of man. Its form remained more or less constant, and only the features and clothing were adapted to conform with the tastes of the time: the European doll was made primarily of wood, terracotta, and

cloth even during the medieval period.

'Image in Rags' was how the doll was known in the *Judiculus Superstitionum* of the eighth to ninth century (A. Fraser in *Dolls*, 1963), and the perishable nature of the materials from which rag dolls were made has resulted in this being the only record of such early specimens.

Nuremberg was a centre of doll production in ancient times, and the city remains faithful to this tradition even today, having extended its manufacture to include toys in general. It was here, in the early fifteenth century, that the first factories went into production to make wooden dolls, representations of which appeared as engravings in the medieval *Hortus Sanitatis* (Magonza, fifteenth to sixteenth century), confirming that this was a thriving craft in the city at that time. The engravings illustrate the craftsmen themselves, like elves with pointed beards and long pointed shoes, working the wood at various stages, from whittling and shaping the rough block to carving, painting, and decorating the final doll.

During the fifteenth century, dolls—mainly produced in wood in central Europe—were made to a high standard and elegantly dressed, often in imitation of the clothes of the owner. They were either articulated in every limb or only above the torso, concealing beneath the skirt a simple cylinder or cone of wood.

We are still a long way from the idea

A German doll-maker at work: an illustration from the *Hortus Sanitatis* of Magonza, which dates from the fifteenth to sixteenth century. The manufacture of dolls in wood was widespread throughout central Europe at this time. Though most were rather crudely made, they had the advantage of being cheap.

Above

A production line in a German workshop making papier-mâché masks and dolls, from an etching of 1698.

Right

of the doll as an everyday object: it was still confined at this time to the children of the aristocracy, while the rudimentary rag doll, a more naïve and poorer creation altogether, continued to be the plaything of children of the lower classes.

In the sixteenth century it was Paris that determined the direction of fashion. While Germany and Holland were by then established as producers and suppliers of wooden dolls, Paris devoted itself to dressing them. The most elegant dolls were dressed in Paris, anticipating a characteristic that really belongs to French dolls of later centuries. Kings and emperors commissioned Parisian craftsmen when they wanted magnificent gifts to delight their children, wives, and lovers. In 1530 Charles V paid ten francs for a Parisian doll to give to his small daughter; Henry II of France commissioned at least six, all for his daughter, and paid nine francs for them. In 1571 Claudia of Lorraine bought six of the finest dressed dolls as gifts for her new-born granddaughter, the future Duchess of Bavaria.

Throughout the seventeenth century, and even more so during the eighteenth century, these ambassadresses of French fashion travelled in jewelled trunks through a Europe torn apart by war, whose frontiers were very different from those of today. In the most splendid courts, those of Spain, Italy,

and England, these dolls were tangible images of high French fashion. Eagerly awaited by ladies of the nobility, who then commissioned new gowns in secret with requests for 'exclusivity,' they provided an efficient means of spreading the word about the fashions of the day. Their fame gradually extended across class barriers, and in order that they should be seen by as many people as possible they were put on show to the public. An example of such practice is to be found in the eighteenth-century Venetian tradition of displaying a doll dressed in the latest Paris fashion for two weeks, over the public holiday to mark the Feast of the Ascension.

One of the earliest English wooden dolls still in existance, which has survived with a complete outfit of clothes. It dates from 1690, and the dress is typical of the period; the enormous beauty spots on its face were all the rage at the time.

These dolls continued to be made in wood, imitating the shape that the aesthetic ideals of the day laid down as the perfect feminine form. The head was oval and rather large in relation to the body, which remained simple, with short arms and, in the finest examples, well modelled hands (normally they were rudimentary) of wood or leather. The legs were generally articulated at the hips, with shoes carved and painted according to the contemporary style. The features were also painted, and all dolls of the eighteenth century had glass eyes with characteristic black pupils. Big beauty spots, exaggerated out of all proportion, were sometimes scattered over their faces in imitation of one of the most widespread fashions of the day.

The doll had acquired an established status that was far removed from its obscure and distant origins. Now it seemed to be inextricably linked to fashion, steeped as it was in the feminine world in which it fulfilled a variety of functions. Marie Antoinette was placated by dolls in the extravagant frenzies that were to cost her her head, and she had her favourites dressed by the court dressmaker, the celebrated Rose Bertin. And dolls served as a 'mirror' in which to try out sumptuous new fashions, jewellery, and hairstyles for those rigidly and dismally ceremonial occasions that were part of court life in Spain, for instance, where every detail of dress had to be minutely observed.

Europe in the eighteenth century, moving towards a series of revolutions that were destined to change its frontiers once more, bequeathed, along with its legacies of culture and history, a clearly defined image of the doll. After the French Revolution and the ensuing idealistic and political upheavals, daily life and children's games continued much as before. Dolls, already favourites with the aristocracy, also began to be enjoyed by children of the poor, though many were to be forgotten and abandoned in dark attics or added to sparse fires in long, cold winters. With the growth of the middle class, dolls moved increasingly towards mass production. From simple, small-scale craftsmanship, their manufacture gradually became completely industrialized, perfectly in tune with the demands of the 'modern age.'

The Grandchildren of Maria Teresa by Johann Zoffany. The essence of aristocratic elegance, the children have been laced into tight jackets and corsets in accordance with the custom of the day. The baby on the chair in the centre holds a stylishly dressed manikin doll with articulated hands and arms.

2
THE GOLDEN AGE

The enormous numbers of dolls produced by craftsmen and industrial manufacturers over the centuries is enough to overwhelm even the most ardent collector. It is absolutely impossible to assess the quantity even approximately, and the most disturbing thought for the real enthusiast is that he will never be able to see the majority of them. This, however, is only one of the collector's anxieties; others, related more closely to the problems of rediscovering and preserving dolls, will be dealt with later on.

The evidence left behind by every generation throughout human history tells the story better than any written material could do. The nineteenth century produced dolls in large enough quantities and made of sufficiently durable materials to be able to withstand not only the damage caused to them by their young owners but also abandonment and, in the following century, the upheavals of two world wars.

We can see clearly the correspondence between the expansion of the middle class and the growth of a semi-industrialized craft responsive to the demands of that new class. The production of toys, and of dolls in particular, increased in order to meet the needs of the children of the powerful and rich middle class, and in the Europe of the nineteenth century the doll took on a formal identity as a toy that was destined for increasingly widespread distribution.

The nations leading the field in this area are easy to identify: Germany, Austria, France, and, towards the middle of the nineteenth century, Britain. Rich in the necessary manufacturing materials——wood and, later, kaolin to make porcelain—these countries determined the appearance of the 'modern' doll. This came about through the establishment of accepted principles of aesthetics, which were based on cultural standards derived from popular tradition, and from constant endeavours to find the 'ideal' doll. From the nineteenth century onwards this search was to encourage competition and to provide a stimulus to improve the prod-

In teaching her doll the rules of etiquette that she had been taught herself, a young girl put into practice the codes of behaviour of polite society and learned them thoroughly.

uct, all this with the aim of acquiring the largest possible slice of the European and overseas markets. It was a real battle, and resulted in a violent clash between the producers in France and Germany, who frequently finished up in court, launching endless accusations of plagiarism against each other and opening the way to the introduction of patents.

An atmosphere of free enterprise and competitiveness led to the great success of the doll industry in the nineteenth century and in the years leading up to the First World War, but the climate of the times then changed dramatically and toy and doll manufacturing was almost brought to a standstill. The increasing shortage of workers and the scarcity of materials resulted in the closure of a large number of factories and caused a decline in the quality of the product of those that survived. The economic problems that pervaded the whole of Europe at the time were of course also responsible for other articles taking precedence over toys in the consumer market.

If one examines today the dolls produced during the last century, which is generally regarded as the golden age of doll-making, one cannot but admire the high level of craftsmanship that accompanied the industrialization of the period, which was in fact a long way from the concept of industry based on total standardization. Every head, even if large numbers were made from the same cast, is different in some small detail, thanks to the skill of the individual decorator. As a result, each one is unique of its kind, and many are real works of art.

Some dolls were inclined to be heavy or awkward to handle because of the techniques and materials used in manufacture, but this often adds to their rather prim dignity, which accorded perfectly with the codes of behaviour imposed on a nineteenth-century middle-class child. Through dolls children learned much about the realities of life, and still do. Customs and manners are often learned indirectly through play, and dolls can serve as modellers of etiquette and as toys with which to act out the lessons taught by adults.

As this historical survey will demonstrate, the doll reflects changes in behaviour and the rules of society, adapting its form and features, using one material rather than another, but always remembering its role as an example to the child.

THE MANIKIN DOLL

The toys of a hundred years ago still manage to enchant us with their innocence, their irony, their good taste . . . in a word, their fascination. Nothing better has been produced since then and it is unlikely that anything will be in future in view of current mass production techniques and the use of plastics. The advertising slogans change from one year to another, but the solid fact remains that the majority of toys are devised and made by adults for their own pleasure. Children simply provide an excuse.

So wrote J. Remise and J. Fondin in *The Golden Age of Toys* (published in 1967) and in this concept lie the roots of the adult doll, a doll based in terms of form and general appearance on an adult woman. At the beginning of the nineteenth century children were encouraged to emulate the adult females around them, and these dolls served as miniature role models. Often of disarming simplicity, they had pretty but inexpensive features, and under the clothes the body was merely a means of support, concealed and in no way physically accurate.

Among the poorer classes, for whom toys existed in a fairly primitive form, the idea of the doll was suggested mainly through dress and facial features. A piece of firewood, an old shoe,

a rag stuffed with straw—anything that could be transformed with a little imagination, a simple dress, and a few rough strokes of paint—could become an object of love and attention. The doll thus took on an almost abstract form, far removed from humanity in appearance and lacking any realistic physical

Manikin dolls of 1800 promoted the Empire style, with its high-waisted dresses, which were in vogue at the time of Napoleon. The size of these dolls, and the elaborate detail of their outfits, made them remarkably lifelike models.

features. It became a sort of symbolic representation of a woman, its body consisting of a shape that resembled the female form just closely enough to be recognized but too crudely carved to be anatomically correct.

Continuous research and the expansion of the industry ensured that in France at least, which led the field in the nineteenth century, the manufacture and accurate representation of the heads and bodies of dolls was steadily perfected. The Second Empire, under Napoleon III, produced superb dolls made of wood or stuffed kid, with jointed limbs. The outline was still that of an adult woman, but the greatest attention was given to the modelling of the heads in the finest porcelain, and the oval faces, the colour of alabaster, had eyes of blue glass. The bodies were no longer rudimentary but, following the strict codes of middle-class morality, they had no explicit sexual characteristics. They left details of the female form entirely to the imagination and concentrated instead on the contours that the fashions of the day demanded. A low-cut dress could not help but expose a smooth neck and bosom, and show off tapering arms and a slender waist, so this much was visible, but the rest remained concealed beneath layers of skirts and underwear. These women in miniature, with whom the young child had such close contact, exerted a pow-

'Girls play with dolls instinctively as a preparation for the duties of motherhood' (Ferriani in *Bamboleide*).

erful influence: girls felt obliged to grow up quickly, and to adapt themselves to the female image that the dolls projected, an image to which they did not themselves naturally relate. Surrounded by an adult world, the child performed actions in play with the doll that imitated those carried out by the mother for her child: she dressed it with care, lacing up its bodice and putting on its crinoline, or whatever outfit was appropriate for the events of the day, and chose suitable accessories, from gloves to fans.

All children talk to their toys; the toys become actors in the great drama of life, brought down to size by the camera obscura of their young minds, and children demonstrate through play their great capacity for abstraction and their enormous imaginative powers. By this means they satisfy their need for creative expression: toys offer the child an introduction to art, or rather to the practical application of art, and no work of art, however perfect, will give rise in an adult to the same fervour, the same enthusiasm, the same certainty. (Charles Baudelaire, *Le Monde Littéraire*, 1850.)

Perhaps in all these mirror games, in which the adult world is reflected, the simplest elements of childhood are lost; instead the child's imagination opens the door to a life of splendid balls, nights at the opera, and receptions at

Fashions for dolls: in the nineteenth century, women's magazines gave a good deal of space to dolls and their outfits.

The wardrobe of an English paper doll of 1800 in the Empire style.

Above

A manikin doll of 1865 in a drawing by Walter Trier.

Left

court. Though the rigours of the social whirl have left no trace of fatigue on the faces of these dolls, their clothes and hair bear all the signs of repeated dressing and undressing, adjustments and readjustments.

By examining the techniques employed in making these dolls, it is possible to appreciate the various stages in their evolution. Let us take as a point of departure the beginning of the nineteenth century, when wood, wax, and papier-mâché were the principal materials used in Europe for making dolls. Making toys and dolls was closely related to the work of the wood-carver, and wood—the most important material—was readily available. Carpenters and wood-carvers would often be asked to make simple toys for children, and as a result a small family business might grow up, with the winter months devoted to the production of toys and dolls and the whole family forming an assembly line, each one responsible for a particular task. In a few cases small private concerns increased their output to the point where they were even exporting dolls to other countries, and publicizing them in printed catalogues with hand-coloured lithographs and captions in German, Italian, French, Spanish, Dutch, and English. We know from the contemporary *Guides to Milan* that one of the most important shops and wholesale dealers in toys at that time was the firm of Maria Berdaner and Sons, which in 1838 had premises in the Corsia del Duomo.

Most of the dolls of this period had heads and shoulders made of wood, and the realism and beauty of their features depended largely on the skill of the wood-carver. The face was generally painted after the wood had been polished and a base of chalk and paste had been applied. The heads were still mounted on very simple bodies, made of cloth in the case of the cheapest dolls, while more expensive ones were made of wood with jointed limbs. They came in all sizes, ranging from a few centimetres to a metre in height. Less refined in style than the rare and highly-prized dolls of the Napoleonic age and the first twenty years of the nineteenth century, whose elegant features were a reminder of their aristocratic associations they are easily identified by their uniformity of style.

The years between 1830 and 1840 saw, alongside the production of toys in wood, dolls with heads of papier-mâché mounted on bodies made of stuffed leather or cloth. These were an innovation in various ways: lighter and more pleasant to handle than wooden ones, they had sweeter faces, brought to life by glass eyes and a mouth that showed a glimpse of bamboo teeth. They combined a more realistic appearance with faster production as the heads could be turned out from a mould and decorated later by hand.

Made originally at Sonneberg in Thüringer Wald, these dolls were exported throughout Europe. (It was in this part of Germany that the first doll-making factories had been founded.) Their papier-mâché heads faithfully reproduced the curls of the current hairstyles, and the finest specimens had curled wigs made of mohair or real hair. The bodies were always fairly stiff, the shoes painted and the wooden arms and legs attached to a stuffed torso. Great attention continued to be given to the head, particularly when, after much research and experimentation by the manufacturers, the use of porcelain was introduced.

The great French and German porcelain companies, such as Limoges, Limbach, and Meissen, as a sideline to the making of domestic articles, began to manufacture dolls' heads; this became recognized around 1840–50 as an established specialist industry. The kaolin used in the making of fine porcelain or china was, like wood, readily available in Europe, and it was used to great effect in these high-quality heads, which combined aesthetic appeal with naturalism.

The processes employed were, for the most part, similar to those of papier-mâché production: china clay was pressed into a prototype mould and was later dried, painted, and fired at a range of temperatures. Depending on whether a clear varnish, a glaze, or a satin finish was applied, and also on the firing technique employed, the result was known either as 'china,' 'glazed,' or 'bisque,' from its characteristically opaque surface.

These dolls became extremely widespread from 1860 onwards. Their features were stiff and their expressions detached, like rather prim and disapproving ladies, and their bodies, generally made of fabric or hide, were very simple and often home-made. The heads were usually bought separately, and for this reason very beautiful heads are frequently found mounted on rudimentary bodies.

A group of German dolls of various sizes and periods made in porcelain. The head in the foreground is of top quality.

The heads themselves were often inspired by celebrated contemporary women who were widely admired and became emblematic figures to young girls of the day. Women such as Eugénie, Empress of France, consort of Napoleon III, were immortalized not only in great court portraits but also in dolls that reproduced their aristocratic features and sometimes their clothes as well, faithfully copying every detail of feathers, ribbons, and bows. Another example was the Swedish soprano Jenny Lind (1820–87), known as 'The Nightingale.' Appointed principal singer to the courts of the Emperor of Austria and the King of Prussia, she had considerable influence on the fashions and tastes of the age and a number of dolls were made in her image.

Produced in bisque so pale that it came to be known as 'Parian' after the white marble from the Greek island of Paros, or alternatively in glazed porcelain, these heads established two highly romantic aesthetic ideals. One type combined blonde hair, done in an elaborate style, with eyes of blue enamel and features that were clearly inspired by Classical Greece; the other matched a mane of black hair with a fair complexion and pink cheeks. The finest examples had eyes of glass, ears pierced by little earrings, and sometimes even jewels or the finest lace around the necks of their *decolleté* dresses. They were extremely beautiful and a very

long way from what we generally think of today as playthings; in fact they are accurate portraits of the fashionable ladies of the day, and as such are of considerable historical value.

Strong links with the fashion world were formed as a result of the rich and elaborate series of outfits with which these dolls were often provided, complete with all the most stylish accessories of the day. Their success increased with the growth of the toy industry in France, which owes much to Madame Calixte Huret and her successors, active in Paris between 1850 and 1920, and to Madame Léontine Rohmer, also based in Paris from 1857 to 1880. Thanks to these two women and their workshops, where much importance was given to the bodies of the dolls and the articulation of their limbs, progress was rapid in the latter half of the nineteenth century and the early part of the twentieth. Patents and continuing improvements led to the establishment of recognized standards in the production of what, in collectors' terms, came to be called manikin dolls, 'poupées-parisiennes' or 'ladies of fashion,' modern names that today identify the 'adult' doll among the vast range of different models produced in the past.

We can now appreciate the extent of the technical innovations introduced by the French manufacturers of this period. In 1850 Madame Huret, as H. D'Allemagne writes in his *Histoire des*

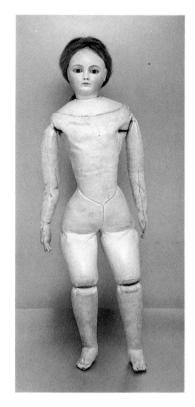

Various types of glass
eyes dating from the
nineteenth century.

Left

An adult doll, probably
made in France and dating
from the second half of the
nineteenth century; height 74
centimetres (29 inches). The
head is bisque and the body
leather, with gussets for the
movement of the arms and
legs. The back is stamped
'Grand Bazar St–Joseph-
Specialité des Jouets; str. S.
Guiseppe Magg. 14–15,
Naples.'

Right

jouets of 1908, began making dolls with heads of bisque mounted on bodies of gutta-percha, a material derived from the latex produced by certain tropical plants. These bodies are fascinating as much for the high level of technical expertise used in their manufacture and the complex articulation of limbs and torso, as for their lightness, solidity and relative unbreakability.

The first patent relating to the manufacture of dolls was issued in 1858 to Léontine Rohmer, to protect her invention of a mobile head, which allowed the head to be rotated right and left. (Until that time the head and body had been modelled in bisque in a single

piece.) In 1861 Madame Huret perfected this concept by setting the head on a neck made in the shape of an egg that rested in a bowl-like container in the upper chest of the doll. Once the two pieces were linked by a pivot, the head could not only be turned right and left but also raised and lowered as desired.

In 1855 the Parisian doll-maker Claude-Joseph Blampoix took out a patent on glass eyes—until then dolls' eyes had always been painted—and thereafter all his dolls bore the initials 'B.S.' (Blampoix Senior) on the side of the chest. Among the oldest Parisian firms specializing in heads was E.

Barrois, which expanded steadily from 1857 onwards, establishing headquarters at 192 Rue St Martin. It claimed to 'specialize in furnishing supplies to the makers of dolls and toys of every kind; heads of dolls in porcelain and bisque of French and German production.' Barrois heads are recognized today by the mark 'E.B.' that appears on the doll's chest or back together with the word 'Déposé' or a number referring to the size of the model. It is important to note that Barrois did not make complete dolls and therefore had to pay other companies (Blampoix and Madame Rohmer, for instance) for the right to use patented articles such as glass eyes or articulated necks.

Another great Parisian firm was François Gaultier, active from about 1860, which made some of the most beautiful of all French dolls' heads and supplied dealers and other companies that made bodies or specialized in assembly or dolls' clothes. For some of the most important clients Gaultier produced heads without the characteristic 'F.G.' on the back so they could be marked with the customer's own trademark.

One of the firms Gaultier supplied was the legendary Maison Jumeau, which had no factory of its own until 1871, when it began making porcelain heads. In 1864, long before it became celebrated, it had patented the design of a wooden body articulated by means of pivots. Bodies of this type were of extremely high quality and were used only for the finest and most expensive dolls; generally they continued to be made of hide or kid stuffed with sawdust and were articulated by means of 'gussets' at the joints.

The competing firm of Léon-Casimir Bru, based in Paris from 1866, also took out a patent in 1869 on a body made of turned wood and articulated at thirteen points. This model (which was also made in rubber) guaranteed movement not only of the major joints but also of the wrists, ankles, knees, shoulders, and elbows.

Certainly a great deal of progress had been made since the appearance of the first dolls with simple heads on crude wooden bodies. By now the Parisian manikin dolls were so finely made and so beautifully dressed that they were selling in the rest of Europe and America as well as in France. They won prizes at the great exhibitions of the period: in London in 1851, P.F. Jumeau won an award for the best dolls' clothing, and again at the World Fair in Paris he won the silver medal, which in 1867 he shared with A.C. Huret; the roll call of illustrious French prize-winners is endless. The dolls they produced, however, are now so rare and so costly that they are beyond the means of most collectors.

THE BABY DOLL

'But tell me, what sort of dolls do you like best? Small ones or big ones? Dolls dressed as babies or as adults? Ones made of fabric, wood or . . .' 'Just dolls to love, please!' (Bettina Ehrlich, *Dolls*, 1962)

There is no doubt that affection plays an enormously important part in all our lives; children are surrounded by it from the first, and they return it without reserve, sometimes too insistently and possessively, as those without the restraint that is generally acquired with social skills are apt to do. In every playroom worn out dolls and threadbare teddy bears lie around exhausted, from the love and attention that is showered on them, having to bear the burden of it in order that children have an outlet for their affections.

The need to love something accounts largely for the huge variety of dolls produced over the centuries and the competition to make them ever more lifelike and lovable. By the middle of the nineteenth century sophisticated 'modern' techniques were being used in the construction of high quality adult dolls or manikins, and French toy manufacturers were continuously engaged in research and experiment in order to expand the market and satisfy customer demand. A new type of doll was invented that was to revolutionize the

industry—the child or baby doll, which is still by far the most popular type today.

Designed initially to represent a girl or boy of up to eight years of age, this new doll resulted from two particular events. At the Great Exhibition in 1851 Augusta Montanari, a highly talented manufacturer of wax dolls, exhibited a series of models representing women of various ages, from infancy to maturity—an idea that won her the silver medal. At the second World Fair, in 1855, François Greffier—a doll-maker working in Nantes between 1844 and 1855—exhibited a Japanese baby doll, which the German firm of Motschmann of Sonneberg used as the model for a doll of its own, with slanting eyes and a generally oriental appearance; it was patented in 1857. This was the start of a new trend that, from the middle of the nineteenth century, was followed by most of the major manufacturers, all striving to produce baby dolls that were more and more perfect and lifelike.

According to A. Fraser (in *Dolls*, 1963), 'the idea of baby dolls is attributable to Montanari and was copied throughout Europe.' It is certainly true that Augusta Montanari was more directly responsible than any other designer for the invention of this new type of doll. She was based in London from 1851 to 1864, and was followed into the business by her son Richard.

These dolls are marked by the liveli-

ness and delicacy of their features and expressions, which are accentuated by their sparkling glass eyes and by the technique developed by Montanari of sewing hair into their wax heads in small clumps using a red-hot needle, which gave them a very realistic appearance. They were made almost entirely of wax—not just the heads and upper chests but also the arms and legs. All the parts were finely modelled and were joined to the fabric torso by means of cords threaded through eyelets.

The advances made by the Montanaris ran parallel to those of another Italian family, the Pierottis. Enrico Pierotti, the son of a manufacturer of religious figures and dolls,

settled in London in about 1790, and by 1853 he was an established doll-maker and trader himself. The two families competed in a race for new inventions, the Pierottis responding to the challenge of the Montanaris' hair technique with an advertisement in which they rather dramatically claimed that hair 'could be repaired as new, and that young ladies could send some of their own hair and get it back stitched into the head of their doll; moreover, the features of the doll's owner could be copied by means of casts.' The Pierotti dolls, although similar to the Montanaris', are not hard to distinguish: Pierotti craftsmen had clearly drawn upon traditional Italian principles of aesthetics in making the lines of their bodies finer and more lifelike. Some sources suggest that the Pierottis' own son was the model for a few of the dolls they produced.

These great manufacturers were not only highly skilled technicians but also the creators of a new ideal: they succeeded in giving the doll a new image, different from the poupée-parisienne not only in the use of materials but also in the cultural links, which were far removed from those of French and German dolls. Of all the countless British and German dolls made in wax, and in papier-mâché covered in wax, those produced by these two remarkable families are undoubtedly the finest.

The manufacture of German-made oriental dolls expanded considerably at

After a stream of dolls looking like rather haughty adult women, here at last were dolls that looked like the children who owned them. This new type of doll dates from about 1850 and resembled children of between five and eight years old. It did a great deal to dispel the rather sinister and disturbing aura that had surrounded dolls until that time.

IL CORREDO DELLA BAMBOLA

I grembiuli figg. 25, 26, 27 si eseguiscono in batista bianca o a fiori con ricchi bordi ricamati in colore o a punto in croce, od anche con incrostazione in pizzo Valenciennes. Gli abitini invece richiedono un tessuto più consistente, come tela bianca o colorata o scozzese, ed anche leggera stoffa di lana. I profilati sono in tinte forti. I bottoni sono preferibili in madreperla bianca.

Il cappellino fig. 22 appartiene all'abito di stoffa verde quadrettata bianco e nero fig. 21. Il rivestimento interno dell'orlo corrisponde al collo ed al nodo della blusa a cintura ed alla gonna pieghettata, attaccata ad un corpetto di fodera.

Il cappello bianco fig. 29, cucito di trine, appartiene all'abito fig. 28, con la cui sottoveste

fare benissimo di lana sottile o filo lucido in base alla forma, figure 51 e 52, andando e ritornando con maglie diritte; il risvolto della manica si farà a righe (una diritta, una rovescia). Una bordura a punto in croce guarnisce la gonna di 65 cm. di larghezza, 40 cm. di lunghezza, aperta dietro e pieghettata fino a + sulle parti che si incrociano posteriormente. Le spalline si fissano con bottoni di madreperla facendo combaciare * su *. Dietro vi saranno dei nastri di chiusura di 65 cm. di lunghezza.

La camicia aperta fig. 37 è guarnita di pizzi; gli orli delle mutandine fig. 38 sono guarniti di bordura lavabile, e le curve, di ricamo, di 26 cm. di larghezza, 2 cm. di altezza; le mutandine hanno chiusura a bottoni e tiro a lacci nell'orlo superiore di 1 cm. di larghezza.

di seta deve corrispondere la guarnizione del cappello tanto pel colore, quanto pei nastri e pei fiori. La blusa di *voile* bianco fiorato trovasi al disopra della gonna a pieghe.

Il grembiule a vestina fig. 44 è di stoffa bleu punteggiata, esso ha delle pieghe tirate avanti che si aprono in basso ed è guarnito di sbieco rosso. La chiusura è a nastrini e lo scollo è guarnito di bordura.

Il grembiule fig. 45 è guarnito di bordura bianca e nera; l'orlo inferiore ha una lista trasversale.

Le mutandine fig. 39 possono essere lavorate ad uncinetto.

Per le vestina fig. 40 la stoffa più adatta è quella lavabile; il corpo è guarnito di un collettone di 3 cm. di altezza e 60 di larghezza, orlato di pizzi; questo collettone si applica, secondo il disegno, con piccolo risvolto e nello stesso modo dell'applicazione superiore della gonna di 8 cm. di altezza, 125 cm. di larghezza. L'altra applicazione — quella inferiore — di eguale altezza e 135 cm. di larghezza.

Le spalle hanno delle alette con sbieco nero e bianco.

I berrettini e le giacchette 34 e 35 si possono confezionare di flanella, panno o simili, con orlo del berretto, collo e maniche ornati di stoffa a grandi punti, in colori corrispondenti alla guarnizione degli altri pezzi e, cioè, rosa o celeste.

La dentellatura ad uncinetto della gonna fig. 36 corrisponde a quella della sotto-giacca che si può

19301. AMBULANCE DE CAMPAGNE garnie de personnages en plomb et d'accessoires en métal peint.

Longueur :	0″40×0″16	0″38×0″24	0″41×0″24
	7.25	**9.50**	**12.75**

19300 NOUVELLE PANOPLIE d'infanterie avec masque protecteur,

avec képi.. .. .. .. 12.25
avec casque feutre 14.75
PANOPLIES Soldats Alliés 8.25
— Officiers Alliés **13.50**

19302. PANOPLIE Officier d'état-major

avec képi 8.50 12.50 16.75
avec képi et fourragère **10.50 17.75**
avec casque métal et
fourragère. .. .. **23.»**

19303. L'AUTO DU GÉNÉRAL, nouvelle auto militaire à traîner, en bois laqué, personnages en bois, articulés et peints.

Longueur 0″42 .. .. .. **10.50**

19304. ALSACIENNE ou **LORRAINE,** poupée dormeuse articulée, costume fantaisie.

Hauteur	0″34	0″36	0″40	0″43	0″47	0″51
	8.25	9.50	11 75	14.25	16.75	20.75
MODÈLE plus ordinaire, non dormeuse.						
Hauteur :	0″28	0″30	0″32	0″35	0″38	0″42
	2 25	2.90	3.50	4 50	5.90	6.90

FAIRE ENTRER LA BILLE DANS LES TROUS DE LA BRANCHE DE LA CROIX DÉFENDUE PAR L'ADVERSAIRE ET L'ON GAGNE

19305. NOUVEAUTÉ " La Croix de Guerre " Jeu de famille très amusant
0″42×0″42
5.90

L'AÉRO BOCHE, FRAPPÉ SUR SA CROIX PAR L'OBUS, TOMBE HORS DE COMBAT !

19306. NOUVEAUTE. 75 contre Aéro Tir à musique cartonnage décoré, canon métal
Longueur 0″53 .. .. **8.75**

LE JOUET LOZÉRIEN

19307. AMEUBLEMENT RUSTIQUE. composé de 5 pièces.
Longueur 0″28. Hauteur 0″15.. .. **5.50**

19308. LA MAISON DU BERGER. personnage et animaux en bois découpé et peint.
Longueur 0″25. Hauteur 0″25 .. .. **6.90**

19309. BERCEAU VANNERIE, garni de cretonne fantaisie.

0″22	0″25	0″30	0″40	0″50	0″60
5.25	5.90	6.50	8.50	11.50	14 50

19310. JOLI AMEUBLEMENT DE POUPÉE en rotin, 4 pièces
12.50

19311. VOITURE BRETONNE en vannerie fine, roues bois, garnie cretonne de couleur.

0″42	0″48	0″55
17.50	**21.»**	**23.»**

Imp. STUDIUM, 22, Rue des Volontaires prolongée, Paris (XV°).

this period. The heads were either mobile or fixed, the eyes were made of glass, the legs and arms were articulated at ankle and wrist, the body was made of fabric and stuffed, and in the stomach was a 'bellows' mechanism that produced a voice. The head was usually made of papier-mâché, and sometimes wax-covered, with painted hair and an appealing simplicity, though the lips were often parted to reveal bamboo teeth which had the effect of dispelling any resemblance to humanity they might otherwise have had.

In 1855 the French firm of Jules-Nicolas Steiner patented a 'mechanical doll that can move its legs, arms and head, and can cry when it is laid down.' It had much in common with contemporary German dolls, but in 1862 Steiner improved his invention, patenting a second 'automatic speaking doll,' which worked on a spring mechanism set into its cardboard torso. The head was made of bisque, but in other respects it closely resembled the earlier type.

Throughout the second half of the nineteenth century the search for perfection continued, particularly in Paris, where in about 1873 Steiner brought out a new model—an articulated doll presented in an ornamental casket. It was around this time that the established and expanding toy-making companies of Paris decided the future of the baby doll by setting a standard for its appearance and manufacture that was to remain unaltered until the last decade of the century. The heads were made of bisque, with a diagonal opening at the nape of the neck for the insertion of glass eyes and any other mechanisms. The hair was generally mohair or real hair mounted on a skull-cap of papier-mâché or cork, the latter a typical feature of Jumeau dolls. Moulds for the heads were in two parts, front and back, and sheet porcelain was pressed into them, though towards the end of the century the porcelain was often poured in a liquid state; this later type is recognizable from the characteristic 'crown' or projecting rim around the two parts of the head, and from the smoothness of the internal surface. Many of the earliest moulded heads, such as those of Jumeau, had ears attached separately, though later ones were generally made all in one piece. Techniques used for painting and firing these heads followed the practices already established for heads in bisque and glazed porcelain.

Bodies at this time were made of wood or papier-mâché and were articulated by means of wooden balls, elastic, and metal springs. It was Steiner who succeeded in reducing from eight to six and finally to four the number of wooden ball-joints as he moved over

A Motschmann doll made from papier-mâché and wax; Germany, 1855–57.

gradually to a new system, in which semicircular joints were built into the limbs, greatly simplifying the processes of production and assembly. This made the bodies much lighter and easier to handle; it also made it possible to achieve perfect articulation of the limbs and opened the way to a whole new range of sizes.

Achievements in French baby doll production were comparable with those of the great Parisian doll manufacturers of the past. The second half of the nineteenth century produced Jules-Nicolas Steiner, Léon-Casimir Bru, Pierre-François and Émile Jumeau,

A wax doll, probably by Pierotti; England, second half of the nineteenth century.

Petit & Dumontier, Alexandre Thuillier, Schmitt, François Gaultier, Jullien, and many others who are generally considered today to have been the greatest of all time.

An army of baby dolls left Paris to conquer the rest of Europe and set off across the ocean to vanquish 'new continents.' They were perfect little images of the ideal child, with enormous eyes, delicate features, a rosy complexion, and blonde curls, and they were dressed in all the rich magnificence of high French fashion, as pristine and elegant as the children of the good middle-class industrial families for whom they were intended, and who would never themselves have thought of leaving the house without hat or gloves. For children they represented another role model, this time much closer to them in age and appearance; they were like sisters who never did anything naughty, were always composed, never played in the dirt, always listened, and hardly ever spoke.

They too were swamped with affection by children eager to give it and undeterred by delicate dresses covered in bows and lace, but there must have

been more than a few 'wise' grand-
mothers who remembered harsher
times and were anxious that an expensive present should not be spoilt; once
the child had had a few moments of
excitement and pleasure, the immacu-
late doll would be packed away for safe
keeping in a lavender-scented box and
only brought out on special occasions.
The fact that the child was forbidden to
play with it and love it freely made it all
the more desirable, but as time went on
it was gradually forgotten. Relegated to
a dark attic, it often outlived its owner,
to be rediscovered and treasured years
later by some other delighted and ador-
ing child. Some of the dolls that survived several generations of children
clearly show the scars today: their eye
sockets are empty, their heads have
been shattered and stuck together with
glue, their clothes are in shreds, but they
are still loved and considered far too
precious to be cast aside for ever.

One French manufacturing firm
more than other was responsible for the
evolution of the doll during the latter
half of the nineteenth century. This was
the Jumeau dynasty, which led the field
between 1841 and 1899. To list all the
great achievements of this firm would
take more than a few lines; F. Theimer
tells the full story in *Le Bébé Jumeau*
(published in 1985), an exhaustive in-
vestigation of the background history
of the firm and its place in the development of doll-making. One thing should

From the mid-1800s the
French baby doll led the field
in Europe and overseas,
establishing a new national
industry. From now on
children could play with dolls
that were doubles of
themselves—pristine,
immaculately dressed, and
perfectly behaved.

'A Child's Paradise,' an English illustration of 1883.

A colour plate dating from the early 1900s showing a doll of the Jumeau type—the sort that every child longed to own, it became a real status symbol in its day.

Opposite

be emphasized: the baby dolls made by Jumeau really are the essence of the great French doll, and their charm and beauty is guaranteed to fascinate even the most detached observer. They were so influential and successful in their own day that they can be regarded as symbols of their age, and certainly as invaluable records of the fashions and aesthetic ideals of the period.

3
THE GREAT FRENCH DOLL-MAKERS

THE BÉBÉ-JUMEAU

Pierre-François Jumeau joined forces with a Mr Belton in 1841, and together they settled in premises at 14 Rue du Salle au Comte, where they pooled their economic resources and founded a doll-assembly firm.

The clothes and the individual parts of the bodies were made by local craftsmen and the heads were imported; made of bisque, the earliest heads were 'whole,' without the characteristic opening that was subsequently introduced to save on weight and customs duty. Some were made of papier-mâché but were in other respects similar to those in porcelain. They were mostly imported from Germany which, as we have seen, was a major producer of dolls' heads. In the early days of the Belton-Jumeau partnership the dolls they produced were not, strictly speaking, French, nor can we ascribe to them precise and distinctive features because they were produced in such variety. The only thing they had in common was their clothes, which were clearly Parisian and won them the bronze medal at the Industrial Exhibition in Paris in 1844. On the strength of this, the firm was commissioned by the Trade Ministry to send a group of dolls to China to show off French fashions.

By 1860 Pierre-François Jumeau was on his own, his association with Belton having come to an end in 1846, and he had moved to 18 Rue du Mauconseil. He made an arrangement to buy heads in bisque from François Gaultier, thus avoiding the problem of importation and ending the search for a more personal product. By 1850 he had invented the 'Bébé-Jumeau,' which was to make his name.

The Bébés-Jumeaux were manikin dolls of fine and medium quality, whose value depended entirely on the richness of their outfits. Jumeau won a number of awards for them, including first prize at the Great Exhibition in London in 1851 and the silver medal at the 1855 World Fair in Paris.

In spite of continuous improvements

This engraving appeared in an English magazine of 1877 with the caption, 'The children's corner at the exhibition celebrating a hundred years of toys and dolls.' The image gives an idea of the quantity and quality of dolls being produced in Europe in the second half of the nineteenth century, mainly by the French manufacturers Jumeau, Bru, and Steiner.

and the recognition that followed them, it was only in 1871, with the opening of new headquarters at Montreuil-sous-Bois, that Jumeau's production became automated. At the same time he opened a factory making porcelain heads, and ensured that they had a personality and individuality quite different from those provided until then by Gaultier.

From 1873 Pierre-François Jumeau was joined in the running of the business by his son Émile, and it was really he who took the leap that opened the way to new industrial methods. Émile also introduced a model that was to become hugely successful and marketed it under his own name, his initials 'E–J' appeared on the nape of the neck of each one.

These were the years in which the Bébé-Jumeau became fully established. It was a period of highly industrialized production, teams of skilled workers being made responsible for the various different components of the doll. There was no shortage of labour, and often teenage girls from the poorest families were hired to work at home for derisory sums. Each one had an allotted task: one person worked only on the moulds for the different parts of the body, one painted the finished article, another assembled the parts. The most skilful were engaged in moulding and decorating the heads. A special section was employed in making the beautiful glass eyes that were the pride of the firm and set a standard that other competing companies tried hard to emulate. Ernestine Ducroix, the wife of Émile Jumeau, was personally in charge of the clothing section, planning and choosing both the styles and the materials.

Such an efficient organization was bound to produce an excellent finished product, and the Bébé-Jumeau's success reflected the genius of its creators. It was made in 17 different models, marked from 1 to 16, with a special doll, marked Number 20, which had a head of 57 centimetres (22½ inches) circumference.

In 1882 Jumeau sold 100,000 dolls; by 1884 the number had risen to 220,000, and by 1897 the production of heads—in white, black, and brown—had hit the three-million mark. The Bébé-Jumeau became almost a national toy, and was patented and publicized as unique and not in any way to be confused with its many imitations. However, though the business continued to expand, there followed a period of problems as a result of plagiarism by other French and German factories; official notices were served and court proceedings began which, in some cases, were to last for years.

To protect itself the Bébé-Jumeau was covered with trademarks and stamps, which still help to distinguish it from the products of its competitors. The nape of the neck was marked with a red stamp, the back with a blue one or, later on, a label; the shoes were stamped on the sole; a band was attached to the arm and a notice was printed on the presentation box: all these precautions ensured that even the most unsuspecting buyer would be aware if he or she had been sold an imitation rather than the real thing. There was in any case a considerable and growing demand for an authentic signed toy: people were no longer satisfied with a beautiful doll but wanted a status symbol as well, which is precisely what the Bébé-Jumeau became.

From 1890 onwards Jumeau dolls were made with lips parted to reveal fine porcelain teeth, an innovation that brought them even greater success. In spite of this fillip, however, this period was the beginning of a gradual decline. Mass production brought about a reduction of the high standards of elegance and quality set by dolls of earlier years, and the factory was beset by problems caused by new laws regarding employees, by strikes, and by a stockpile of materials in the warehouse as a result of fierce competition from German firms, which managed to maintain low prices and high productivity.

In 1895 Pierre-François Jumeau died. In his last years the firm was plagued by conflicts over patents and suffered not only from competition both at home and abroad but also from the political situation in France. It ceased mass production in order to avoid further accumulations of stock and began, almost as its swan song, to produce a few top quality models in papier-mâché

The consequences of fame: an advertisement in *The Youth's Companion* offers not a true Jumeau doll but one 'made after the celebrated Jumeau model.'

Our New Jumeau Pattern Doll, Eléna.

Given for one new name, and 25 cts. additional.

Fair Eléna

presents her card, and we take pleasure in introducing her to our young friends, who, we know, will be delighted to welcome her.

As she cannot speak English, she will say a few words in French, which we will translate. "I am a thousand times happy to greet you all. You have been such good friends to my cousins, Reta, Adele and Felice, that I know we shall have delightful times together.   ELÉNA."

The Doll Age is the growing age. It is the age in which habits are formed. With a pretty Doll, habits of industry, of neatness and of order can be established.

As we give with the Doll a set of Paper Patterns, a little girl can soon learn (in an amateur way) the art of dressmaking.

Is there a little girl without a love for Dolls? Whether it be of Wax or Rags, of China or Wood, still her heart yearns toward it, and she delights in tending and caressing it.

To Be Encouraged.

We believe this affection should be increased rather than in the least discouraged. Time spent with Dolls is not time thrown away. We are glad that we are still able, as in the past three years, to offer our girls a Doll well worthy of all the love and care that can be lavished upon it.

The Doll Age is a happy age—there is no doubt about it. Much does a pretty Doll contribute to the happiness of this age. Unfortunate must be the little girl who has never owned a Doll. Children of all nations, whether savage or civilized, take equal delight in this universal toy.

The Kitchen Set and Dishes.

All given for one new name

This Set consists of a nice Stove and Furniture, and about 50 useful Tin Dishes, Tea Kettle, etc., etc. The cut gives you a little idea of the variety. No Rolling Pin goes with this Set. This premium is about double the value of the one given last year for one new name. We give the entire Set for one new name. For sale by us for 90 cts. Postage and packing, 40 cts., when sent as a premium or purchased, or sent by express and charges paid by receiver.

Description.

Our new Doll differs from those previously offered by us. It is made after the celebrated Jumeau model, having the ball and socket joints at the elbows, shoulders, knees and hips, also joint at the neck, so that the head can be turned naturally. It has a beautiful Bisque Head, with "Natural" Eyes and flowing Hair of a most luxuriant growth.

Its Lips and Teeth.

This Doll is unlike others with simply a painted mouth. Its lips are beautifully moulded and slightly parted, showing pearly porcelain teeth which have been naturally inserted. They are charming. The Doll is dressed as seen in the cut, and is 16 inches high.

Paper Patterns.

We also give with this Doll a Set of Paper Patterns, with directions for making her wardrobe. These Patterns will enable a girl to do her own cutting and fitting, and will prove to be a most delightful and instructive occupation.

Given for only one new name, and 25 cts. additional. Price, $1.25. Postage and packing, 65 cts., when sent as a premium or purchased. This Doll is larger and much heavier than any of our former Dolls This accounts for the heavy postage charges. We suggest that when you order the Doll either as a sale or premium, you request us to send it by express, not paid. In most cases it will cost you less by express than by mail.

FELICE.—We have in stock a quantity of the Doll Felice, offered by us last season. Felice has a Kid Body and Bisque Head.

We still offer her for one new name, and 20 cts. additional. Price, $1. Postage and packing, 40 cts., when sent as a premium or purchased.

Child's Decorated China Tea Set.

No. 72½. 23 Pieces. Given for one new name, and 10 cts. additional.

This is the largest and prettiest Child's imported Tea Set we ever used. Each piece is beautifully hand-painted in colors, with gold lines. The Set consists of 23 pieces— Tea Pot, Sugar Bowl, Cream Pitcher, 6 Plates and 6 Cups and Saucers. The Tea Pot is 5 inches high, and other pieces in proportion. All packed in a wooden box. Given for one new name, and 10 cts. additional. Price, $1. Sent by express, and charges paid by receiver, when sent as a premium or purchased.

according to the old and expensive production methods of its early years. The heads were made by pressing porcelain into moulds, with the ears attached separately, and the faces were given a range of different expressions, numbered from 200 to 220 (but excluding 213, presumably because of superstition); they came in a selection of sizes numbered from 9 to 12.

These dolls are fascinating not only for their high quality but also for the innovative spirit that inspired such character and individuality. Their great success prompted the German manufacturers to follow in their footsteps from about 1900 onwards with the 'bébé caractère' in an attempt to produce dolls of their own with as much personality.

On 10 March 1899 the story of the Maison Jumeau, and of many other Parisian factories, came to an end with the forming of the S.F.B.J.—the Société François des Bébés et Jouets—in a final attempt to fight off foreign competition and survive as a group. Unfortunately the dolls produced after the formation of the S.F.B.J. were not of the same high quality as before, and standardization was to lead to a general shoddiness that ultimately brought about the slow decline of the great French doll-making industry.

THE LUXURY DOLLS OF LÉON-CASIMIR BRU

Opinions on the subject of beauty are constantly changing, and though much discussion may be devoted to good and bad qualities, a conclusion will never be reached. The first impression on looking at a doll made by the French manufacturer Léon-Casimir Bru, however, is that it is indisputably beautiful. Its remote, almost rapt, expression with a hint of a frown, the intense look in the eyes that seem always to be gazing into the distance, and the slight smile on the half-closed lips, all contribute to its astonishingly lifelike and fascinating beauty.

The fundamental difference between the Bru and the Jumeau dolls is that the

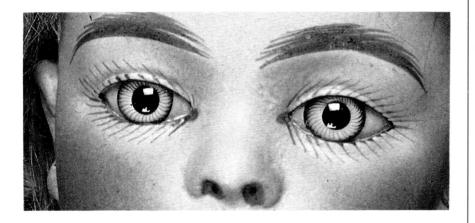

The unmistakable dreamy eyes of a Bru doll dating from the 1880s.

dolls made by Bru were luxury items, and were sold as such, with guarantees of excellent quality and superb finish. Léon-Casimir Bru and his son were based in Montreuil-sous-Bois from 1866 to 1883, and when Casimir Bru *Jeune* took over the management in 1875 the company became firmly established and began to expand. After the introduction of the baby doll, Bru brought out a luxury model with a fully articulated body made of wood, thereby rejecting the current trend towards papier-mâché and composition bodies. In 1879 they took out a patent on a new doll, which was to be their greatest success. Its proportions were carefully worked out—the size of the head had to be one fifth the height of the body, its egg-shaped neck rested on shoulders made of bisque, and the rest of the body was of stuffed hide. (Later models had forearms of porcelain.) It was usually marked on the nape of the neck with a small circle and a spot, a half-moon or sometimes the letter 'B.' The body was later improved, particularly in its articulation, which until then had been fairly limited.

Henri Chevrot, who succeeded Bru *Jeune* in 1884, had taken out a patent the previous year on a body made of hide with greater movement in the hips, arms made entirely of bisque, and legs of porcelain jointed at the knee. From 1886, however, the legs were made of wood as porcelain proved to be too fragile.

The most remarkable of the baby dolls produced by Bru had the characteristics common to them all but certain exclusive features in addition. They were marked 'Bru-J.ne' on the nape of the neck, while the back, the arms (which bore a size reference number), and the chest were all stamped and labelled. Expensively and elegantly dressed, they sold at a higher price than the dolls produced by other companies, but nonetheless found a ready market with the rich upper and middle classes.

They won the silver medal at the Paris fair of 1878, at Melbourne in 1880 and Anvers in 1885, and the gold medal at Paris in 1889, where they were described as follows: 'The Bru dolls are the only ones with realistic eyelashes. They are also distinguished by the fineness of their hands and feet and by the beauty and good taste of their clothes.'

The management of the factory changed hands again when Paul Girard took the reins, concentrating on perfecting the technical aspects of the models already in production. This was the period of the company's greatest financial success and expansion. Later, as we have seen with Jumeau, competition from Germany began to create problems at the Bru factory, where production costs were particularly high. A period of simplification began in which the manufacture of dolls with bodies of hide was suspended on economic grounds. Girard turned his attention to making traditional baby dolls with bodies of wood or composition and standardized heads with less

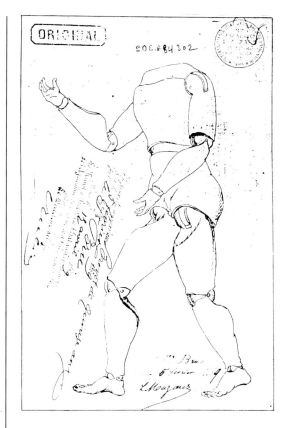

Two original Bru patents: *above* the doll with a rubber body, which dates from 14 August 1878; *below* the 'Poupée Surprise, whose head turns to show two faces, one awake, the other asleep' (9 December 1868).

character in their faces. Slowly the fall in quality affected sales and Bru too was absorbed by S.F.B.J., though their trademark continued to be used for a few more years.

THE FACE OF THE STEINER DOLL

Jules-Nicolas Steiner, who worked in Paris from 1855, was perhaps the most creative of all the great French doll-makers. As well as producing many patented mechanical inventions, and improving construction techniques to make dolls larger but lighter, he devoted his efforts to creating faces of greater character and diversity. Foreseeing the potential success of the baby doll, he was aware of the commercial strength and the competition offered by such firms as Jumeau, Bru, and Schmitt, to whom he responded by immediately releasing on to the market baby dolls with a variety of faces, marking them with the initials 'A–B–C–D' preceded by 'Fig.re.' He also produced a series marked 'G–FC–FG', but examples are extremely rare and found only in museums and private collections.

Steiner dolls have charming, chubby little faces, their mouths either closed or open to reveal two rows of teeth (this latter type, model B, is known as 'The Shark' in collectors' jargon). The trademark appears on the hand or the body, with a stamp or a label, depending on the year of production. A characteristic feature of the Steiner dolls is the special violet-coloured cardboard used in making the body (and also sometimes the skull), which was extremely light in comparison with traditional materials.

In 1878 the firm was awarded the silver medal at the World Fair in Paris for its 'mechanical speaking doll.' In 1881 M. Bourgoin joined the company, and in 1888 he was appointed director. Many of the Steiner dolls of this period have the words 'Bourgoin-succ.' stamped on the rim of the head, a trademark that is often mistakenly associated only with dolls with movable eyes (controlled by a lever at the nape of the neck), whereas in fact it was also used for models with fixed eyes that continued in production.

In 1889 the company won the gold medal at the Paris fair for its baby dolls, which were advertised as 'unbreakable,' and in the same year it registered a trademark in the form of a label showing a doll holding a banner printed with the words 'Le Petit Parisien,' which was applied to the front of the torso and replaced the blue die-stamp.

In 1890 the management of the firm passed unofficially to Amedée Lafosse, an appointment that was confirmed two years later. Behind the scenes, however, Jules-Nicolas Steiner still kept an eye on his factory, which was by this time a real competitor to Jumeau. Other dolls made around this time, improved versions of earlier models, appeared under the names 'Bébé-Liège' and 'Poupée-Merveilleuse' (1899).

In 1900, under the guidance of its new manager, Jules Mettais, the company

A Steiner doll of 1867. Its head is made of bisque with fixed blue glass eyes. The lips are parted to show two rows of teeth, which has earned it the name of 'The Shark' among collectors. A spring mechanism inside the cardboard body enables the doll to move and cry (see also photograph on page 183).

began to produce ethnic dolls—mostly black and mixed race—but, despite its attempts at innovation, Steiner, like Bru and Jumeau, slowly began to lose ground.

OTHER GREAT FRENCH MANUFACTURERS

The three great Parisian doll-makers already discussed may have dominated the market, but there were many other French firms who produced very beautiful high-quality dolls, some of which were copied by the larger companies while others remained individual and brilliantly imaginative in their detail.

Among them was A. Thuillier, whose factory was operative from 1875 to 1890, making dolls in hide or wood and composition; heads were made of bisque and marked with the initials 'A-T' and the reference number of the size. They are now considered to be among the most beautiful of nineteenth-century dolls and are great rarities today, much sought after and very expensive.

Petit & Dumontier, another manufacturing company, was active between 1877 and 1890. Little is known of them except that they made dolls with wide, flat faces and eyes rather close together, which made them look like Pekinese dogs. It was this firm that, in 1877, patented the use of a metal alloy in the articulation of the wrist to avoid breakage of the fingers.

Schmitt & Fils (1863–91) also deserves mention among the great French firms, having won awards and accolades for the quality of their dolls at various international exhibitions. Their products were beautifully made, with anatomically accurate bodies articulated by means of eight wooden ball-joints. They were generally marked on the back with a shield containing the initials 'SCH' surmounted by two nails in the form of a cross. Schmitt & Fils also produced baby dolls, with bodies made of gutta-percha and jointed by means of pivots, which only rarely appear on the antique market today. The bisque heads were so beautifully made and so distinctive in character that they are very highly prized by collectors.

Doll manufacture was not, of course, confined to the great French firms of Jumeau, Bru, and Steiner. Throughout France small toy-making businesses flourished, constantly inventing and promoting new models.

'What better gift could there be than this delightful doll?' wrote the women's magazine *Petite Echo de la Mode* in December 1892, illustrating its special offers to subscribers. This particular model was undoubtedly inspired by the dolls produced by Jumeau.

Opposite

DEMANDEZ PARTOUT
LE BAMBIN
NOUVEAU BÉBÉ INCASSABLE
ARTICULATIONS BRÉVETÉES S.G.D.G.
IL SE TIENT DEBOUT, ASSIS & A GENOUX
ET FAIT TOUS LES MOUVEMENTS HUMAINS
MÉDAILLE D'OR (DIPLÔME et 1ᵉ CLASSE) A L'EXPOSITION de LONDRES 1890
LA DERNIÈRE PERFECTION du JOUR

Puppenschule

LA PAIX EST SIGNÉE !!

La leçon d'écriture; écrivez avec zèle

Studi Artistici

Moneglia, Stab. Civicchioni - 437

4
GERMAN GENIUS AND
THE BÉBÉ CARACTÈRE

In their own particular world, French baby dolls were the greatest triumph of the late nineteenth and early twentieth centuries, and their success triggered off an explosion whose effects spread far beyond the confines of France. Thousands of doll-making firms throughout Europe set out to imitate them, not always with good results, and generally speaking their copies or variations on the French theme offered very little competition on grounds of either aesthetics or quality.

Germany, however, had a long tradition of toy-making, and responded to the challenge of France's expanding industry by uniting its experience in porcelain manufacture with the expertise of its craftsmen and its economic strength. Though its early dolls succeeded in maintaining a fairly high standard, they were not in the same class as French ones of the period. German baby dolls borrowed only their basic structure from the French, eliminating everything inessential or expensive to manufacture, and in the process they lost all that was most fascinating

about the dolls produced by the great French companies. With a few exceptions, the bodies were anatomically rudimentary, the heads uniform in style and not always of very high quality, and the clothes simple and typically German. But as a result it was possible to keep prices low and competitive, and to succeed in markets where French dolls were beyond the reach of most people.

Germany achieved enormously high production levels, but quality varied greatly because of the disparity between the technical methods employed by large factories and those used by small family workshops. Some long-established firms, followers in the best national traditions of toy-making, achieved a large output without allowing quality standards to fall, and began supplying dolls' heads to other manufacturers both at home and abroad. Simon & Halbig, based at Gräfenhaim in Thüringer Wald from about 1870 to 1925, are a case in point. One of the oldest manufacturers in Germany, this firm made good quality dolls of all sorts, at first in hide and later in papier-

'Googlie,' one of the most famous 'bébés caractères.' Although it was a caricature in some respects, there were definite similarities with a real baby—in the roundness of the head and eyes in particular—which contributed greatly to its success, just as they did with some of Walt Disney's creations.

Italian, French, and German postcards showing parallels between the lives of children and their dolls.

Preceding pages

mâché and wood, articulated by means of elastic. Their heads were well made and were often supplied to other reputable companies, such as Kämmer & Reinhardt and Heinrich Handwerk. They were also used by Cuno & Otto Dressel for their models No. 1349 and 'Jutta,' by Fleischmann & Blödel for their 'Eden-bébé' and by Gimbel Bros for their model No. 500. Simon & Halbig heads can also be found on bodies stamped with the trademarks of Jumeau and of Roullet & Decamps, demonstrating that their success extended even to France, the motherland of the doll.

Another well-known name is that of Armand Marseille, also of Thüringer Wald, who had a factory at Köppelsdorf from 1865 to 1925. Every serious collector must have encountered at least one of his dolls; pretty enough to be instantly appealing, they had naïve, typically German faces with healthy, rosy complexions, and they came to symbolize the German doll throughout the world. Similar in every way to other contemporary dolls in terms of construction, Armand Marseille's model Nos. 370 and 390 were typical examples of the bisque doll of the period.

The firm of Heubach (1881–1925), which produced a vast range of different models, cleverly adapted the skills of traditional craftsmen to the needs of modern industry and expanded their manufacturing empire throughout Germany. They specialized in baby dolls of a traditional and individual character and, like many other earlier and smaller firms, established themselves in the field of the bébé caractère which, with the beginning of the new century, was to turn the doll-producing world in a new direction.

THE NEW TREND

The year 1900 began in a blaze of light: fireworks, bonfires and champagne toasts were accompanied by the optimism that always greets new beginnings.

Industrialization led to rapid change in every area of life, including behaviour, morals, taste and dress. Dolls adapted swiftly and flexibly as the era of opulence and extravagance that had produced the poupée-parisienne came to an end; even the French baby dolls, with their layers of lace and their dreamy expressions, rapidly began to lose ground. Girls wanted dolls that reflected their own times, and from this new demand grew the great success of the bébés caractères, which were made principally in Germany between 1900 and 1915.

The term refers to a specific type of doll, either male or female (its sex was defined by its clothes, which were either pink or blue), representing a newborn baby, or a baby only a few months old, with a distinctive and recognizable expression on its face—a smile, a scowl, a look of surprise or contentment—which gave it a particular character.

In the first few years of this century, a group of designers and doll-makers in Munich (among them Marion Kaulitz) began to make dolls that were accurately modelled on real babies. Not all were pretty and some were positively ugly, but for the first time children could relate to them as lifelike images rather than aesthetic ideals. There is no doubt that *en masse* these bébés caractères present a rather alarming spectacle, their faces twisted into every conceivable expression and fixed forever in cold porcelain, but individually many of them have a great deal of personality and charm. They were an instant success. As the German toy industry entered a new age, they became its principal product. They were part of a movement towards realism that was firmly based in the social structure and morality of Germany, and they helped to bring about an expansion of the industry and a new emphasis on naturalism. They won the hearts of thousands of children who wanted to play with a doll and express their love in a freer way. Fed up with images of ideal babies whose behaviour and appearance they were supposed to emulate, children found in this new doll an informal and undemanding companion.

The new century moved fast, requiring flexibility and an instant response on the part of industry to the changes that were taking place. While doll manufacturers kept pace with technical advances, however, they also had to bear in mind the traditional needs of children for toys on which they could lavish affection and, in the case of girls, practise their maternal skills.

In the nineteenth century dolls representing babies had been made in Germany in wax, papier-mâché, and bisque, but they had had little success. Now German manufacturers returned to these early models and improved them. In terms of general construction, the bébé caractère followed tried and tested technical principles; the body continued to be made in papier-mâché and the style was simply adapted to suit

The rosy-cheeked dolls of Käthe Kruse became the subject of a series of postcards whose captions were translated for the various countries in which they were sold. This is the Italian version of one card in the series.

Grandi pensieri.

57

current demands. One can still find dolls of this type today, with bodies made up of five parts—torso, arms, and legs—articulated at the shoulder and hip joints, and modelled on newborn babies. Other types, known as 'toddlers' in collectors' jargon, were made of more parts and had more elaborate articulation so they could stand up straight.

Some models were constructed very simply, with bodies in stuffed canvas, which made them pleasantly soft to handle, and sometimes with a mechanism that produced a voice. Their heads were made of bisque and, later, of

Ich mache Einkäufe für Mama.

Another card from the Käthe Krüse series. The German caption reads, 'I am doing the shopping for Mummy.'

celluloid; wax was by now very much on the decline.

The wide variety of models on the market—new ones appeared all the time to keep up with competition and changing trends—led to certain adaptations in the structure of the heads. To save time and money, they began to be made with moulded and painted hair and with eyes that were sculpted and painted as part of the porcelain head instead of the traditional glass eyes inserted separately. The mouth continued on the whole to be made with the lips parted to show the teeth, but in some cases—among them Kämmer & Reinhardt's Nos. 101, 109, 114, 115 and 117—the mouths were closed. The open or closed mouth, therefore, gave no certain indication of the date of manufacture, as it had done in the past with traditional French and German dolls.

Armand Marseille brought out a highly successful and inexpensive model known as the 'Dream Baby,' which represented a baby with its head already covered in downy hair and its mouth half open to reveal two teeth. The body was made either of fabric, with the hands in celluloid, or—in the larger models—of composition. On its neck it bore the number 351, together with the trademark of the company and the number of the size. The same doll with its mouth closed was numbered 341. Around 1924–25 Marseille produced a huge series of newborn 'caractère' dolls, but his greatest success was the 'By-lo Baby,' designed by the American Grace Story Putnam, who took out a copyright on it in 1922, two more in 1923, and a fourth in 1925.

The search for the perfect model for the bébé caractère led to the examination of hundreds of newborn babies at a Los Angeles hospital, the final choice being a three-day-old baby who became the model for a German prototype head made in bisque; it was exceptionally naturalistic and lifelike, and, even by today's standards, its commercial success was enormous.

The mainstay of the German doll industry was the firm of Kämmer & Reinhardt, which was in operation from 1886 to about 1925 at Waltershausen in Thüringer Wald. From 1895 it used the letters 'K–R,' with a star and six dots between them, on all its heads. Many of the most beautiful 'caractère' dolls carry this mark, sometimes alongside that of Simon & Halbig. In 1901 Kämmer & Reinhardt registered the trademark 'Mein-Liebling' for a doll that was to become one of their most profitable ventures. Numbered 117, it represented a baby with a rather worried and thoughtful expression. In 1901, model No. 100, known simply as 'Baby,' came on the market; referred to by collectors as the 'Kaiser-baby,' it has a face that cannot be described as beautiful, but it

undoubtedly has character. In 1910 Kämmer & Reinhardt began making a series of baby dolls that have now become celebrated: 'Carl,' No. 107; 'Elsie,' No. 109; and 'Hans and Gretchen,' No. 114, took their places beside 'Peter and Marie,' No. 101, which were already in production, and the great model No. 126, which is considered by collectors today to be the finest the firm ever made.

In the first two decades of the twentieth century, the quality and variety of bébés caractères, and of the factories involved in producing them, increased to such an extent that it would be

Permetta che io le presenti . . . .

impossible to catalogue accurately all the individual models manufactured at this period. If a particular doll was not a success, the mould would be set aside or destroyed and production of the model

Another Italian card, this one reading, 'Allow me to introduce you to . . .' Even the world of dolls had its etiquette.

would cease, another one replacing it immediately. As a result it is occasionally possible to find dolls today that are almost unknown, even in the field of collecting: Kämmer & Reinhardt's No. 6 was made in such small quantities that examples of it are extremely rare, and when one was auctioned at Sotheby's recently it fetched an astronomical sum.

Several generations of dolls also emerged from other famous factories, such as J.D. Kestner, Kley & Hann, Baehr & Proeschild, C.M. Bergmann, F. & W. Göebel, Bruno Schmitt, Franz Schmitt & Co., Schoenau & Hoffmeister, and Theodor Rocknagel. A wave of exoticism in the fashion world produced a series of bébés caractères of many races and skin colours—black, brown, yellow and white. Many of them, the most successful among them, were based on live models and accurately reproduced the characteristics of the race they represented. The buying public was by this time extremely demanding and shrewd: people had become used to keeping pace with rapid changes of fashion and to the assimilation of new ideas, and they were discriminating in their choice of dolls from a selection that was constantly altering and expanding. The days were long gone when series dolls could merely be tinted, as Bru, Jumeau and Steiner had believed, in order to persuade the public that they represented babies of different races.

Characterization was the winning card, and as time went on it became accentuated almost to the point of caricature: one example of this is the 'Googlie' doll, which bore more resemblance to a cartoon character than a baby, but nearly all the German manufacturers moved over gradually to this exaggerated version of the bébé caractère. There were variations on the theme, but generally speaking these dolls had round faces with wide eyes looking to the side and a smiling mouth that was often suggested rather than accurately drawn.

One particularly successful model was the 'Kewpie' doll, designed by the American Rose O'Neill, whose trademark was registered in the United States in 1913. It was made entirely in bisque, with a very appealing face, and was articulated only at the shoulders, so the arms could move but the body was stiff and the legs joined together. It was not so much a traditional doll as a mascot or toy that could be invested with any sort of significance its owner chose to give it. It was widely distributed in a whole range of materials—rubber, celluloid, and wood among them—according to the demands of the market in different areas, and it also appeared in a black version. It inspired a series of unauthorized imitations (in Italy it found its alter ego in the 'Cirillino' doll made by Ernesto Peruggi), and it even became the heroine of stories and cartoons.

Via Vincenzo Monti, 32 - VITTORIO BONOMI - MILANO - Via Vincenzo Monti, 32

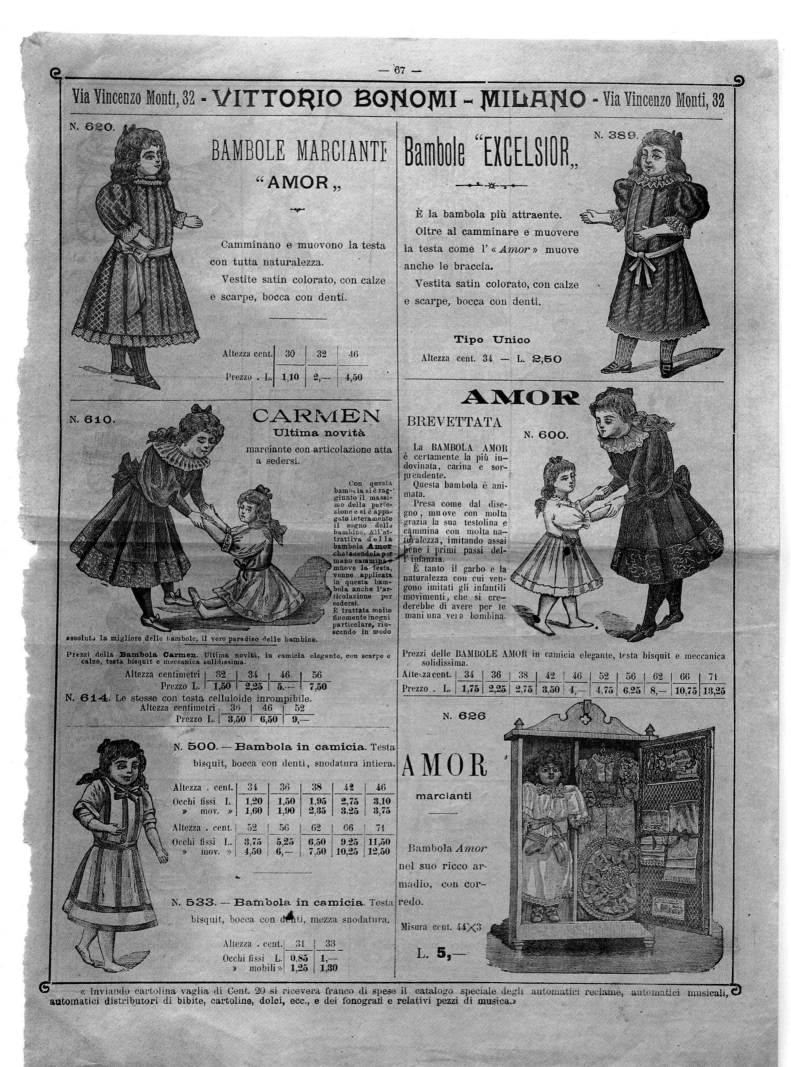

N. 620.

BAMBOLE MARCIANTI
"AMOR„

Camminano e muovono la testa con tutta naturalezza.

Vestite satin colorato, con calze e scarpe, bocca con denti.

Altezza cent.	30	32	46
Prezzo . L.	1,10	2,—	4,50

Bambole "EXCELSIOR„

N. 389.

È la bambola più attraente.

Oltre al camminare e muovere la testa come l' «Amor» muove anche le braccia.

Vestita satin colorato, con calze e scarpe, bocca con denti.

Tipo Unico

Altezza cent. 34 — L. 2,50

N. 610.

CARMEN
Ultima novità

marciante con articolazione atta a sedersi.

Con questa bambola si è raggiunto il massimo della perfezione e si è appagato interamente il sogno delle bambine. All'attrattiva della bambola **Amor** che tenendola per mano cammina e muove la testa, venne applicata in questa bambola anche l'articolazione per sedersi. È trattata molto finemente in ogni particolare, riuscendo in modo assoluto la migliore delle bambole, il vero paradiso delle bambine.

Prezzi della **Bambola Carmen**. Ultima novità, in camicia elegante, con scarpe e calze, testa bisquit e meccanica solidissima.

Altezza centimetri	32	34	46	56
Prezzo L.	1,50	2,25	5.—	7,50

N. 614. Le stesse con testa celluloide inrompibile.

Altezza centimetri	36	46	52
Prezzo L.	3,50	6,50	9,—

AMOR
BREVETTATA

N. 600.

La BAMBOLA AMOR è certamente la più indovinata, carina e sorprendente.

Questa bambola è animata.

Presa come dal disegno, muove con molta grazia la sua testolina e cammina con molta naturalezza, imitando assai bene i primi passi dell'infanzia.

È tanto il garbo e la naturalezza con cui vengono imitati gli infantili movimenti, che si crederebbe di avere per le mani una vera bambina.

Prezzi delle BAMBOLE AMOR in camicia elegante, testa bisquit e meccanica solidissima.

Altezza cent.	34	36	38	42	46	52	56	62	66	71
Prezzo . L.	1,75	2,25	2,75	3,50	4,—	4,75	6,25	8,—	10,75	13,25

N. 500. — Bambola in camicia. Testa bisquit, bocca con denti, snodatura intiera.

Altezza . cent.	34	36	38	42	46
Occhi fissi L.	1,20	1,50	1,95	2,75	3,10
» mov. »	1,60	1,90	2,35	3,25	3,75

Altezza . cent.	52	56	62	66	71
Occhi fissi L.	3,75	5,25	6,50	9,25	11,50
» mov. »	4,50	6,—	7,50	10,25	12,50

N. 533. — Bambola in camicia. Testa bisquit, bocca con denti, mezza snodatura.

Altezza . cent.	31	33
Occhi fissi L.	0,85	1,—
» mobili »	1,25	1,30

N. 626.

AMOR
marcianti

Bambola *Amor* nel suo ricco armadio, con corredo.

Misura cent. 44×3

L. 5,—

5
THE INVENTION OF THE MECHANICAL DOLL

The desire to animate dolls so that they more closely resembled people had its roots in the very distant past. Petronius, who lived at the court of Nero in the first century AD, spoke of a doll made of silver that was capable of imitating the movements of a human being. We cannot check his claim, but there is no doubt that man was seen as the absolute master of the animal world and that there were many attempts to challenge the act of creation; the possibility of giving life to an inanimate creature made by man would put him almost on a par with the gods that ruled him.

Moving on to relatively recent times, extraordinary mechanical creatures were made in the eighteenth century that seem to have descended from space or mythology. This was the period when a fashion for the bizarre and exotic swept the richest courts in Europe in a search for novelty and entertainment; it was an age when art and science made adventurous and triumphant strides yet much seemed still to be veiled in mystery and magic.

Between 1768 and 1774 Pierre-Jacques Droz, a Swiss clockmaker, together with his two sons, made the famous 'androids' that can be seen today at the Museum of Art and History in Neuchatel. These strange creations are among the most disturbingly naturalistic mechanized dolls ever produced. Two of them represent boys, the third a young girl. The first, known as Charles, is the 'Scribe'. He can write a message up to forty letters long, and then, having dipped his quill pen in an inkwell, leave a space and begin again. The second, Henri, is the 'Draughtsman,' and he can produce four different pencil sketches: a child with a butterfly; a puppy; a portrait of Louis XV; and profiles of George III and his wife, Charlotte of Mecklenberg. The third 'android' is, however, perhaps the most fascinating: it represents a pretty young girl playing a miniature organ. She plays five tunes, her head turning to left and right as she follows the movements of her fingers on the keyboard. A mechanism worked by bellows makes her chest rise and fall so

The Milanese firm of Vittorio Bonomi described their dolls in eloquent terms in their catalogue: No. 600, patented under the name 'Amor,' was claimed to be 'so natural in the way it imitates a child's movements that one would think one was holding a real child in one's hands.' After a lot of walking it could have a rest, like No. 626, 'in its elaborate wardrobe, complete with trousseau,' which sold for five lire.

that she appears to be breathing, and she is capable of such a complex series of head movements that the result is astonishingly realistic. Her name is Marianne, in memory of Droz's wife, who died young. These creatures do seem very real and yet their endlessly repeated movements, calibrated to the last centimetre, paradoxically underline man's limitations as the creator of life.

Other legendary names from the past are well known today, but sadly few of the weird and wonderful creatures they invented still exist. Jacques Vaucanson became famous, between 1737 and 1741, as the inventor of a series of remarkable automatons, among them a duck that imitated to perfection the movements of a real duck, and could peck corn and 'digest' it; by a chemical process the food was eliminated in what appeared to be the normal way. In 1778 Wolfgang von Kempelen made an automatic chess player, and it is said that in 1809 Napoleon lost a chess game playing against it; perhaps the emperor was not a good player, but certainly he was unaware that inside the robot's control box a man sat watching all his moves through a series of mirrors and directing the robot to make the appropriate responses.

In the nineteenth century, manufacturers turned their attention to technical and mechanical devices that would provide dolls with a few more

basic human functions. Research was directed primarily at creating a voice that could reproduce the words 'Mama' and 'Papa'. The first mechanisms, which were fairly rudimentary, were based on a system of bellows made of leather or parchment fixed in the stomach of the doll and worked by drawing in air and letting it out again with a squeak when pressure was exerted and released (it would still be quite a while before any words would be heard). This device was in use by the early 1800s and remained unchanged throughout the century for most of the less expensive models on the market: those made by Motschmann, for example, and some dolls made in wax and papier-mâché.

A children's journal, *Le Bon Genie*, reports that at the French Industrial Exhibition of 1823 there were dolls on display that said 'Maman' if one touched their right hand and 'Papa' if one touched the left, an invention that was patented by Maelzel in 1824. An advertisement of the time stated: 'Pour six francs je remue les yeux et je tourne la tête. Pour dix francs, je dis Papa et Maman.'

A more sophisticated mechanism worked on a spring that allowed the doll to cry 'Mama' if held upright and 'Papa' if laid down on its back. The automatic speaking doll of 1862 already referred to, which was patented by

Steiner, is an example of this type. Still striving for perfection, Steiner took out another patent on a voice system in 1892 under the direction of Lafosse. These devices, generally made in a light metal, bear the name of the firm, thus helping to identify the origins of certain antique dolls that have no external markings. The voices of many dolls, especially those that date from 1870 onwards, were operated by two cords threaded through the sides of the doll's body and attached to a mechanism inside; when they were pulled the doll said 'Mama' and 'Papa.'

Great attention was given by Maison Bru to the voices and animation of their luxury dolls. In 1867 they registered a patent for a 'Poupée-Criante,' which is believed to have had the features of an adult, and in 1872 Madame Bru patented a 'Bébé-Surprise,' which probably had a body of wood, metal, or rubber and contained a musical box. This great firm marketed a series of ever more perfectly automated dolls, using the bellows system to produce their voices, as did most other companies of the period. In 1895, under the management of P. Girard, a new patent was added to the many others already registered by Bru: it was for an automatic baby doll that could speak, 'breathe,' and close its eyes.

From 1885 Maison Jumeau had been following the trend towards speaking dolls, using the bellows and cords sys-

Also from the Bonomi catalogue, 'Clowns playing the cymbals. This magnificent colourful toy is worked by turning a key to wind up the clowns, who then beat their cymbals together.'

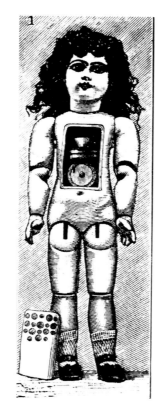

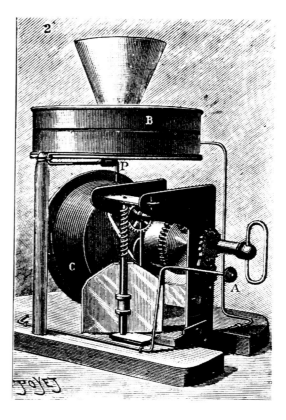

tem, but Emile Jumeau's interest in developing this idea still further was greatly stimulated by Edison's invention of the phonograph, which was first exhibited to the general public at the World Fair of 1889. Jumeau saw that its potential could be adapted to improve the range of sounds that dolls were capable of producing. There were, however, certain problems to be overcome, such as the competition offered by other companies. Maison Stransky, who for example, used the Edison system to produce a 'Poupée Phonographe Merveilleuse,' which was on the market from 1891 to 1894, just at the time when Jumeau's own doll was available. Jumeau collaborated with the clockmaker Henri Lioret to make the 'Bébé Jumeau Lioretgraph,' which appeared in its final version in 1893. It corresponded in size to a No. 11, and it had parted lips and a voice system that could produce whole sentences of about sixty words on a variety of topics, depending on which disc was inserted.

If, to the joy of those present, dolls could manage to say a few words between incomprehensible wailing noises, surely they were also capable of much else. One of their most important accomplishments would be to open and close their eyes in simulation of waking and sleeping—part of everyday human life and therefore expected of dolls for their young owners to regard them as babies with needs and impulses similar to their own.

Towards the end of the nineteenth century a few dolls in wax, or in wax-covered composition, were fitted with simple devices that could be activated by means of a cord threaded through the body and connected to the eyes: when the cord was pulled the eyes closed. These were, however, fairly unsophisticated systems that could not be guaranteed to work perfectly or to last long. Many of the dolls of this type that have survived now have empty eye sockets or rather sinister-looking squints. It was again the French manufacturers who took the lead in developing technology in this area: having already been responsible for the famous 'human eyes' in glass, which were such a feature of their early dolls, they produced some fascinating solutions to the problem of eye mobility.

Steiner registered three patents, two in 1880 and one in 1881, for devices that moved the eyes by means of a small metal lever at the nape of the neck. The eyes were highly individual: the irises were made of glass in a variety of colours and set into a lozenge of white porcelain, which was joined by metal pivots to a wooden bridge placed laterally inside the head and attached to the operating lever.

Jumeau patented a number of different systems, including, in 1885, one that closed the eyelids, similar to that registered by Léon-Casimir Bru in 1882. Because of the amount of space between the eye and the eyelid this was not altogether an effective system, though the device was improved in 1886. A patent of 1887 covered the movement of the eyes alone, which now had eyelashes and were operated by a metal 'butterfly' or small pivot at the nape of the neck. The patent of 1896 finally simplified this system, a rocker arm making it quieter and more efficient than before.

Closing the eyes by means of a lead rocker, which worked on gravity (the position in which the doll is held controls the rolling of the eyeballs), became the most widespread and commonly used system among all French and German manufacturers. Swinging the eyes from one side to the other in what was known as 'flirting' worked on the same principle, and was used with some success in a few models produced by Simon & Halbig.

By this time dolls could speak and even play the coquette but, not content with that, they attempted something even more difficult—walking on their own. Only a few succeeded. Not many dolls could stand upright unaided and

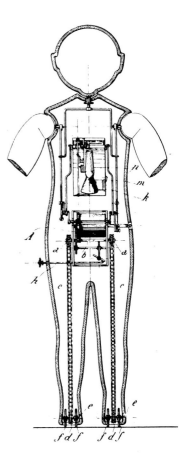

The mechanism of the walking doll produced by Fürther Puppenfabrik Fleischmann & Bloedel in 1895.

even for them it was only possible to glide—rather than walk—on wheels fixed into the soles of their feet. Among the best known was the 'Autoperi-patetikos,' patented in 1862 in Europe and America by Enoch Rice Morrison. Their rather basic metal bodies were wisely hidden under full dresses and surmounted by heads in clear porcelain or parian, with sculpted and painted features and hairstyles. Others, for example those made in Paris by Alexandre-Nicolas Théorude between

1842 and 1895, managed to 'walk' by means of a spring mechanism that activated a device hidden under their long petticoats. A simplified system was operated by cords attaching the legs to the head, which allowed one leg to move in front of the other and the head to turn in time with the steps. This method was widely used, even in the earlier part of this century, for inexpensive dolls of average quality.

A sophisticated mechanism operated by clockwork was patented by Steiner in 1890, for his 'Bébé-Premier Pas'; it was simplified in 1893 but continued to be used for speaking and walking dolls.

Jean Roullet and Ernest Decamps, who became associated in 1889, marked their mechanical dolls with the initials 'R-D,' which appear on their patent of 1886. In 1893 they produced a highly successful walking doll known as 'L'Intrépide Bebe,' which was operated by an extremely efficient clockwork mechanism and imitated perfectly the walking action of a human being.

Maison Bru also followed the trend and, on the initiative of P. Girard, produced a 'Bébé-Petit Pas.' Among their many innovations designed to make dolls as naturalistic as possible was the famous 'Bébé Têteur,' patented in 1879; a rubber container inside the head even enabled it to drink milk from a bottle. The first of this type had heads made of bisque on wooden or composition bodies provided by Steiner, as

A mechanical sedan chair carried by flunkeys; Vichy, France, c. 1865.

appeared on the original patent. Advertisements of the time also refer to a 'Bébé Gourmand' which could eat and 'digest'; there are some doubts, however, about the details of the patent, and preserved examples of the doll itself are so rare as to make it almost impossible to evaluate. Maison Bru's 'Poupée-Surprise,' which first appeared in 1867 and was improved in 1868, had faces on both sides of its head with different expressions, one crying and the other smiling, or one awake and the other sleeping. The head could be turned by hand on a pivot to face whichever way the child chose. This 'multi-face doll,' as it came to be known by collectors, was a great success and many German factories adapted Bru's idea for mass production. One such manufacturer was Carl Bergner, who flooded the market in 1904–5 with his doll with three faces; it was constructed in a way similar to those made by Bru, and was marked with a blue die-stamp and the letters 'C-B' on its torso.

By now the doll could do practically everything, or at least everything required by a well-brought-up child: it could laugh, cry, walk, sleep, sing nursery rhymes, suck a bottle, and even blow little kisses with a turn of its head. At times all this proved a little too much, making the doll difficult to handle and very delicate, and family tragedies often occurred as a result of a fall by a precious walking doll left momentar-

'The Jolanda doll imitates a child's first steps,' from an Italian catalogue of 1901.

ily unattended. Heads were sometimes broken beyond repair, and mechanical devices ceased to function because of the heavy demands made on them by actions as simple as walking and sleeping. Who knows how many children, tired out after playing rather nervously with their precious but temperamental mechanical doll, festooned with ribbons and endlessly prattling, would not have preferred to lock it away in its special box and curl up instead with a soft, undemanding teddy bear!

EUGENIE
und ihre Garderobe.

Eugenie
et sa garde-robe.

EUGENIA
and her wardrobe.

6
PROMOTERS OF FASHION

Among the many aspects of the French doll that have earned it universal acclaim are the quality and elegance of its clothes. The French toy industry had specialized since the very beginning in the finer points of fashion and all its accessories, and it had no equals in this field. The clothes of French dolls corresponded precisely with those of contemporary adults, reproducing every technical and stylistic feature in the minutest detail.

As the fashion capital of the world, Paris was a magnet for all women who wanted to be well-dressed and up-to-date, and the doll—an expensive and ephemeral object in itself—was well suited to the task of advertising French fashions, its widespread distribution among the middle and upper classes making it the perfect publicity vehicle. It was impossible to mistake it for the product of any other nation, and 'Parisian doll' became synonymous with chic to even the most discriminating French fashion buyers.

Until the eighteenth century the primary purpose of the poupées paris-iennes was to act as promoters of fashion, but with the advent of printed magazines and fashion figurines at prices accessible to a far wider public, the doll began to lose ground as a fashion model. As we have seen, however, the vast majority of dolls produced until the 1870s continued to represent adult women, and of these many performed the functions of both plaything and miniature fashion model. This was a direct result of the richness and elegance of their clothes and accessories—and of the extent of their wardrobes, which accurately reflected the real needs of a contemporary woman of fashion. By 1807 Parisian commentators were reporting that dolls were 'very well dressed', their elongated lines imitating the Empire style dresses that were so fashionable at the time. In *La code de la mode* (1886), H. Despaigne wrote:

A woman of the world who wants to be properly dressed at all times has clothes for every occasion: seven or eight changes of dress for the day would include a dressing-gown for

Trademarks of some of the firms that specialized in fashionable dolls' clothes.

the morning, a riding habit, an elegant house robe for luncheon, an outfit for walking in the city, another for carriage visits, dresses for walks in the Bois de Boulogne, for dinner, for the evening, for the theatre. This is no exaggeration, and her wardrobe was further extended by the need for swimming costumes and beach clothes for the summer and hunting and skating outfits for the autumn and winter, if the lady wished to share these healthy pursuits with the men.

Until the early years of the twentieth century, children's clothes were still strongly influenced by those of adults, of which they were often replicas in miniature, complete with all the features that made them restricting and uncomfortable. Girls were brought up to model themselves on the adults around them and to make themselves 'beautiful and desirable', and corsets and crinolines encouraged them to feel like little ladies at a very young age. The joys of infancy and childhood were denied almost entirely in the rush to grow up and join in the social rituals of middle-class life.

In 1846 King Louis Philippe of France gave Princess Victoria Adélaïde, daughter of Queen Victoria, a doll with a magnificent wardrobe consisting, as the label confirms, of outfits for the morning and the evening, two ball gowns, a dress in the finest gauze, embroidered jackets, a scarf, satin shoes, feathers, bonnets, hats, corsets, jewellery, underwear, and an Indian cashmere shawl, which was the height of fashion at the time.

Natalie Rondot, describing the sumptuous wardrobes of some of the dolls exhibited at the World Fair in Paris in 1867, wrote: 'These toys are not really intended for the very young. They are made for rich customers who wish to buy an expensive present for a woman, and use her children as a means of doing so.' This observation clearly underlines the dual role played by dolls at the time.

One of the principle French factories, involved not only in making heads but also in assembly, was Maison Barrois. An inventory dating from about 1849 contains the following information on the stock in its shop: '500 m. of Indian cotton, 480 m. of muslin, 25 m. of black tulle, 200 m. of white tulle, 25 m. of jaconet, 20 m. of velours for bodices, 100 m. of batiste in various colours.' And this was by no means a complete list of the materials required to dress these little 'ladies' correctly. An industry grew up specifically to serve their needs: the easy availability of underpaid manual workers, willing for a few centimes to risk losing their sight sewing by candlelight, helped to build up profitable businesses specializing in clothes for dolls just as already existed for the manufacture of adult clothes.

There were milliners, hairdressers, even florists for dolls, makers of fine underwear, leather gloves, shoes, and accessories—such as fans made of lace, painted ivory, or wood, parasols, and, of course, jewellery.

The great French dress designers were well aware of the importance of the doll as a fashion promoter and, though less than before, continued to use it as a publicist: the three elegant manikins in the Museum of the City of New York were dressed by Charles F. Worth in his heyday, around 1860–70, when he was dressing the Empress Eugenie. But dolls such as these, which travelled with trunks full of the latest French fashions wherever they went, were clearly in the minority: most were rather more modest and, though fashionably dressed, had less extensive and exclusive wardrobes, and it was these models that were normally on sale to the general public through large department stores. Once their clothes were out of date, however, even the magnificent poupées-parisiennes finished up as the playthings dolls were originally intended to be.

One example of a luxury doll of the late nineteenth century, with a wooden body and bisque head, and almost certainly attributable to Léon-Casimir Bru, can be seen at the Museum of Isola Madre on Lake Maggiore. This manikin still has a superb collection of clothes, including walking and evening dresses and fine embroidered and monogrammed underwear. A court cape confirms the traditional belief that the doll had been made for the House of Savoy and that, once the splendour of the court had faded, it was treated with rather less respect than before; most of its wardrobe has unfortunately been lost as a result, along with all the elaborate accessories it must once have possessed.

'Mourning clothes for widows and orphans,' an illustration published in *Margherita* in October 1885. The 'orphan' consoles herself with a manikin doll dressed in the very latest style.

The expansion and distribution of fashion journals, which helped to promote all areas of the adult clothing industry, were matched by a similar growth in magazines aimed at young people, which—in addition to offering edifying advice on behaviour along with sentimental clichés—included paper patterns for dolls' clothes and hats with instructions on how to make them and embroider and decorate them. There were articles on fashions for dolls and lists of addresses from which young readers could order the best accessories as well as the dolls themselves. Not surprisingly, many of these magazines were produced by well-known doll-manufacturing companies. One of the most successful was *La Poupée Modèle*, which dates from around 1863; owned by the company that published the popular women's periodical *Journal des Demoiselles*, it had hand-painted illustrations and the same stylish image. Other journals of a rather more modest type included the *Gazette de la Poupée* of 1865–6, run by Mlle C. Huret, a well-known designer of dolls, and their clothes and accessories. Apart from the usual articles offering advice and various services, it was above all a means of publicizing the manufacturing firm that owned it; much of it was devoted to serialized stories about a doll called Huret, which was marketed by the parent company.

As well as magazines and manikin dolls, there were also paper dolls available at this time that were designed to be cut out and dressed in a whole range of different outfits. They were widely popular during the nineteenth century, though in concept they dated back to the early seventeenth century in Germany and around the 1790s in England, having been intended from the outset as a means of promoting fashion. They were easy to distribute and cheap to produce, and mothers and children could share in the fun of cutting them out and changing their clothes. Among the most famous was 'Psyche,' which was a great success in the first half of the nineteenth century. It was followed by many others, some very grand, some less so, but quite often representing famous women from history such as the Empress Eugénie together with her sumptuous wardrobe, all packaged in cardboard or wooden boxes.

The history of these paper cut-outs follows almost exactly the development of three-dimensional dolls. In the latter half of the nineteenth century, in response to popular demand, paper dolls imitating babies began to appear, accompanied by a wave of publicity aimed at securing a large share of the market. From the mid-1870s onwards their success steadily increased while the popularity of manikin dolls began to fall away.

Fashion outlines changed dramatically in this period—the crinoline was

The bustle begins to take over from the crinoline.

76

replaced by the bustle—and at the same time interest began to develop in the area of baby clothes. French dolls had the reputation of the Paris fashion world to live up to, and they clearly reflected this new emphasis. The heyday of elegant dolls' clothes, this was also the time when the two distinct sectors of the French doll industry—baby dolls and manikins—came to be clearly defined and recognized. The most stylish poupées-parisiennes were those produced by Mlle Huret, followed by Barrois, Blampoix, Simmonne, Jumeau, and Bru. Under the careful guidance of Ernestine, the wife of Émile, the firm of Jumeau achieved a standard of quality that has never been surpassed. Many of their baby dolls were sold completely dressed, others simply in a nightdress or slip which allowed children to dress them as they wished, according to fashion and the resources of their parents, an idea that proved very popular. Under Ernestine Jumeau's direction, about three hundred new models were produced every year, each one finished in a slightly different way or dressed in a different range of materials—always perfectly in

The fashion-plate doll was also a wife and mother, as this etching illustrates.

keeping with the fashions of the day—so that each had its own individual character. Their popularity was increased by their claims to be the best-dressed dolls of their type, 'without equal.'

But dolls' clothes began to follow the slow decline that had already been seen in the manufacture of the dolls themselves towards the end of the century.

By 1900 the great days of opulence and extravagant taste were already gone, but many German factories nevertheless continued to send their dolls to France to be dressed: the legend lived on despite the decline, though careful scrutiny of the dolls' clothes of the period clearly reveals a lack of quality in the materials used and in their cut and styling, though this was often cunningly concealed by quantities of lace and ribbons.

In 1905 a new journal, *La Semaine de Suzette*, which was aimed at eight- to fourteen-year-olds, came out in France. Anyone subscribing for a year was sent a doll 25–30 centimetres ($9\frac{7}{8}$–$11\frac{3}{4}$ inches) tall, produced by S.F.B.J. and called 'Bleuette'; its success story was to last over fifty years. Paper patterns were published regularly in the magazine to allow young readers to dress their doll themselves, and were presented like the fashion plates issued by the great design studios of the Rue de la Paix; from the

Twenties onwards, they were the work of a team working under Mme Langereau, the wife of one of the editors of the magazine. About 350 designs were published in a booklet under the title *Le Trousseau de Bleuette*, which came out twice a year to coincide with the summer and winter collections. Each season five or six new styles were added and a few others dropped, and, as in the world of high fashion, they were given names such as 'Charmeuses,' 'Un Souffle,' and 'Sans-Façon.' They were also provided with all the appropriate accessories that contemporary fashion decreed.

The great success of *La Semaine de Suzette* ensured that Bleuette acquired a brother, 'Bambino,' and a big sister, 'Rosette,' both with extensive wardrobes. Bleuette finally disappeared from the scene in 1960.

The dolls of this period were strange, narcissistic creatures, very much a product of the society that bought and sold them, but we must not forget that for better or worse they were the ancestors of the dolls of today, and that we have to move on a very long way to find firms that could compare in terms of quality with Huret and Jumeau, or could produce dolls like Bleuette who revived the tradition of the 'doll of fashion' with such remarkable success.

THE AGE OF CONSUMERISM

The idea of a plaything that was also a work of art, to be treated with care and respect, was by now a thing of the past. Twentieth-century dolls can all be defined as 'modern' in their overall conception because they were made essentially as toys and were produced in response to consumer demand; as a result they cornered a large share of the toy market. Lower costs made it possible to replace them when they got broken, and children, increasingly aware of all that was available in the shops, constantly cried out for something new and different. This is the sort of chain reaction that has become an accepted part of our consumer society.

The last great years of the toy industry, when toys of real quality were still being produced, marked the frontier between two worlds and two disparate ways of life. The period disrupted by two world wars was one in which every new endeavour was frustrated by shortages and fraught with problems of communication, and for many people the difficulties affecting business initiatives were insurmountable. Doll-manufacturing firms inevitably suffered the same fate as other industries, along with a large part of the society they had been developed to serve.

In a Europe that was slowly recovering from the horror and butchery of the Second World War,

basic manufacturing materials were exhausted and most factories had been closed, destroyed, or adapted to other uses. It was the end of an era for the old Europe. Across the Atlantic, however, there was an abundance of wealth, youth, and dynamism. America's optimism was the panacea that a depressed and impoverished Europe badly needed; it offered luxuries and light-hearted pleasures, and had the money to support the consumerism that was to make these the 'boom years.'

The history of the doll reflects very clearly the spirit of brash enthusiasm and immediacy of post-war America. This was the great age of Hollywood and of a new freedom for women. The new symbol of the age was blonde and slim and made of indestructible plastic—a typical product of a rich and frivolous world; she was a 'pin-up' doll in a bathing costume, with a ponytail, and she was called 'Barbie.' The new generation of children adored her. She was the all-American girl: instead of promoting the names of prestigious designers, her clothes were made for a life of disco dancing, skiing, surfing, and sailing. She was part of a world in which the glamorous ideal was not an evening of romantic waltzes but of cocktails in a Manhattan penthouse. Good taste, especially in clothes, has always been associated with France and Italy, but 'The Look' was typically American and Barbie personified it.

The American Barbie doll led a fashion parade in which dolls all over the world took part. Always in tune with the times, she wore a classic one-piece bathing costume for her first appearance in 1959, but by 1987 she had become as flashy and glittering as a movie star.

Buon Natale

S.1326/3

7
THE ITALIAN SCENE

Even the most determined researcher has a problem identifying more than a few toys and dolls of a specifically Italian character, especially at the time of the great success of France and Germany in this field. In spite of their widely recognized skill in working with wood, wax, ceramics, and papier-mâché, Italian craftsmen tended to concentrate their efforts on areas other than toy-making.

The Italy of the nineteenth century, caught up in one of the most crucial upheavals of its history, was little more than a geographical definition and certainly had no political identity. One factor, however, was constant: religion was still a powerful influence in the lives of working people, especially in the south, and the craftsmanship of the period was clearly inspired by it, as it had been for centuries. While the doll industry reached its zenith in other parts of Europe, statues of a healthy young Madonna with a rosy-cheeked Baby Jesus continued to pour out of Italy.

Toys and dolls were of course pro-duced in some numbers but the middle and upper classes tended to buy imported ones, which often came into Italy in separate pieces to save on customs duty and were then assembled and dressed by local distributors.

The birth of a truly Italian doll came only in 1870, and was the result of a meeting between Luigi Furga Gorini, a wealthy landowner with capital to invest, and a craftsman by the name of Ceresa. Ceresa had recently returned from Germany, where he had worked in a factory making papier-mâché masks, and Furga decided to launch a similar business with him in Italy. As the sale of masks was limited to the carnival season in early spring, however, Furga began making papier-mâché dolls' heads as a sideline (the technical processes involved were similar), but the results of the early series were rudimentary and offered no real competition to those available on the international market. They had painted features and were made in one piece, their crudely modelled bodies hidden beneath very simple dresses. They measured about 12

'While dolls are well dressed, there are many children suffering from the cold,' declared *Bamboleide* in a moralizing tone in 1895. There is no doubt that at least until the Twenties, the doll was a luxury object that only the well-off could afford.

to 14 centimetres ($4\frac{3}{4}$ to $5\frac{1}{2}$ inches) and cost only 60 centesimi a dozen wholesale (10 centesimi each to the general public).

By 1888 Furga was a member of the Chamber of Commerce, Industry and Crafts, with a factory at Canneto sull'Oglio in the province of Mantua. His production of dolls rapidly expanded, continually improving in quality, and his heads in both papier-mâché and wax began to compete with those from France and Germany, thanks largely to the manual skills of the women employed in the factory. But in spite of his high standards, it was a losing battle: these were the years in which France produced its most beautiful bisque dolls, and fashion decreed that heads should be made of porcelain. Furga resorted to importing heads from Germany, where production costs were naturally much lower, and proceeded to mount them on his own papier-mâché and composition bodies.

In 1918, largely as a result of the uncertainty that imports from abroad would ever arrive, Furga's daughter, Carlotta Superti Furga, initiated the production of bisque heads at their Lombardy factory which freed the firm from dependence on foreign suppliers. From this new venture was to emerge a model that is known to every collector; on the nape of the neck it is marked 'Furga-Canneto sull'Oglio,' together with the size number.

These were, generally speaking, dolls of medium quality, all with similar facial characteristics (perhaps because there were relatively few of them made) and they are easily distinguished from their French and German counterparts. They were made in various sizes, up to a metre (3 feet) in height, and they had simple articulated bodies; a small number, about 30 centimetres (12 inches) tall, were made in fabric stuffed with straw, with bisque arms and without a joint at the neck. The eyes were either fixed or mobile.

The 'caractère' baby dolls made by Furga are of even greater interest, and were decidedly superior in quality; though the German influence is apparent. The clownish 'pagliacci', with their painted faces, are delightful.

After the porcelain factory closed in 1928, Furga gradually increased its doll production, but only in the years following the Second World War did the company achieve real independence and sufficient individuality in terms of style and characterization to be recognized on an international level.

Other small Italian factories followed Furga's example towards the end of the nineteenth century, and some remained active until about 1940: there are known to have been factories in the Mantua area that made bisque heads, others in Florence that specialized in unbreakable papier-mâché dolls, and a number in Milan, Brescia, Como, and

Varese. Evidence of one such factory is provided by 'caractère' baby dolls similar to Simon & Halbig's model No. 126 and marked '1361/38—Attilio Cortinovis—Como Italia'; there are also bisque heads for dolls and decorated heads for 'pagliacci' in existence which bear the words 'Bollate,' 'Antenore,' and 'Made in Italy.' One name to remember is that of Mario Franco, who was based in Turin and registered a patent in the United States and in Germany for a method of making rag dolls.

In the Veneto region, small doll and toy factories flourished in Venice, Verona, and Udine, and from the toy factory in Fagagna, Friuli, in operation from about 1891, a few documents and toys have survived. The Countess Cora Savorgnan di Brazzà gave new impetus to the firm by importing original German toys, especially stuffed animals, from 1904 until the factory finally closed in 1918.

The manufacture of stuffed animals, puppets, and dolls derived largely from the availability of cheap skilled female labour and the tradition of mothers making dolls for their children at home. The endeavours of two women, Margarete Steiff and Käte Krüse, were mainly responsible for raising production levels in this area and organizing small-scale enterprises along more industrial lines.

One manufacturer of fabric dolls was

Elena Konig Scavini, who began a small business before the First World War and, once the war was over expanded it with her husband, Enrico Scavini, into a commercial operation. Based in Turin, it took as its motto 'Ludus Est Nobis Constanter Industria,' the initials of which—LENCI—became the trademark of the company. Success was not long in coming: almost immediately the popularity of the Lenci dolls spread beyond Europe to America, where they became instantly fashionable. They were made in soft cloth and dressed with great care and elegance in stylish colours, always using the same materials, and never losing their distinctive and characteristic originality. The American magazine *Playthings*, which

Two Furga dolls of about 1920, made entirely in bisque.

'Mignonette,' made in porcelain by Furga from the early 1900s until about 1920.

Dolls from the Lenci catalogue, showing some of the many brilliant creations of the only Italian firm to have contributed significantly to the industry.

Preceding pages

promoted them in the United States, described them in October 1920 as 'dressed in a great variety of styles and brilliant colours; there are Indians, Cowboys, Harlequins and a whole range of other attractive models.' They were marketed under the name 'Scavini Dolls.' The same magazine announced the new trademark of 'Lenci di E. Scavini' in November 1922, the year in which it was registered in Italy and Great Britain. The success of these dolls grew at such a rate that the sales of traditional models soon considered out of date, suffered considerably. It became every child's wish to own a Lenci doll, though it was a wish that often remained unsatisfied because they were far from cheap; partly because of this, perhaps, they were considered suitable presents for grown women as well as for children. Some actually represented 'femmes fatales' in rather seductive poses, and were clearly intended to be

displayed on silken couches or in the centre of a sumptuous bed.

In April 1923 *Playthings* warned its readers to be sure to buy dolls marked with the original Lenci trademark in order to avoid confusing 'Lenci dolls, famous all over the world and made in Turin by Italian artists' with the huge numbers of imitations that were being passed off by other manufacturers as the real thing. Competition came from smaller firms on all sides who were eager to profit from Lenci's success and produced inferior copies at lower prices; two such firms were Guacci and Alma.

The trademarks of the Lenci dolls varied according to the model and the year of manufacture. Among the earliest marks was a metal button, which was usually attached to the underwear, and bore the name Lenci. Then there was a blue die-stamp on the soles of the feet, which was in general use from 1930

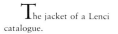

onwards. Little cotton tickets (later replaced by cardboard ones) with the name of the firm and the number of the model were stitched into the back seam of the doll's dress.

Alongside its expanding production of dolls, Lenci began making high-quality ceramics under the same trademark, producing an exceptional variety of articles in collaboration with a number of well-known artists, such as

Mario Sturani (1906–78) who worked with them from 1932 and designed beautiful ceramics, furniture, and dolls.

Lenci dolls were unmistakably Italian, independent of any foreign influence and faithful to the best national traditions of originality and craftsmanship. In 1950 the Lenci factory changed hands, but it still produces dolls today of a type and quality similar to those that made it famous.

8
ART AND THE DOLL

The most fascinating thing about a doll is its face, and no amount of technical ingenuity in the construction of its body, sophisticated mechanisms to make it perform, or sumptuous clothes can make up for a face that lacks character and charm. This must have been perfectly understood by nineteenth-century manufacturers, who were catering to a market that laid great stress on female beauty and its social importance. Many dolls of the period were a synthesis of contemporary ideals of femininity, both infant and adult: blue eyes were matched by golden curls, raven tresses by hazel eyes and pink cheeks, and in terms of deportment these Parisian dolls seem to have been raised with the same iron discipline as the children of the time.

In time, however, the beauty of the dolls produced by most of the French factories became so uniform as to be rather characterless and flat, which had a damaging effect on both the image and the sales of dolls. While Steiner anticipated this problem, as we have seen, by producing models with a range

of different faces, Jumeau tackled it by making his dolls even finer and more exquisite, and turned to the world of art for inspiration. He was convinced that it was vital to make dolls with personality, and in the sculptor Albert-Ernest Carrier de Belleuse (1824–87), whose work was highly regarded, he found a willing collaborator. Together they designed a new type of doll, known today as the 'Jumeau triste,' 'Long Face,' or 'Cody Jumeau,' which was instantly successful. The first two names derive from its long sad face and the third is a reference to William Cody, alias Buffalo Bill, who visited Europe in 1887 and bought one of these dolls for his little daughter. They first came on the market in 1879 in sixteen different sizes: numbers one to eight had ears moulded in one piece with the head; numbers nine to sixteen had ears attached separately. The heads were all made in pressed bisque. Unfortunately, very little precise or detailed information on these dolls exists, and no special promotional material was produced at the time. Their heads were not marked with

'The first essential is that the artist creates images; if there are no images there are no ideas, and civilization slowly but inevitably dies.' (Herbert Read, *Art and Society*). The beautiful example of a 'Jumeau triste,' *opposite*, is an image of such imagination and subtlety as to be a work of art by any standards.

any distinguishing code numbers, except for one relating to size. Since Jumeau had his finger firmly on the market's pulse and was never reluctant to publicize the qualities of his famous baby dolls, the complete absence of any signature or initials on the heads is very curious, particularly since they were modelled by a well-known sculptor. The heads were usually mounted on Jumeau bodies bearing the stamp 'Jumeau Medaille D'Or,' which at least defines their origin. This type of doll, widely sold between 1880 and 1885, was undoubtedly one of the finest examples of all the Jumeau baby dolls.

Among other artists who worked in collaboration with doll-makers, a place of honour must go to Albert Marque, a sculptor who was active in Paris towards the end of the nineteenth century. To him we owe a doll's head of great character, datable to about 1905: it is a remarkably lifelike representation of a little girl, with a tip-tilted nose, big thoughtful eyes, and a heart-shaped mouth. The sculptor's name appears on the nape of the neck. Today it is one of the rarest of all antique dolls and is much sought after by collectors.

In the early years of the new century there was a marked increase in the dolls

A detail of the 'Jumeau triste' that appears on the previous page.

The trademarks and signatures of some of the artists who designed the faces of French dolls of the period.

Opposite

designed by artists, perhaps in an attempt on the part of the French manufacturers to give them an even greater delicacy and finesse and so outdo the Germans, whose sales were definitely on the increase. They were also anxious to discover some new element that would breathe life into a market that was by this time a little tired and lacking in dynamism.

The design of the dolls made by Lanternier of Limoges was entrusted to two artists, the portraitist Edmée Masson, who produced 'Cherie' and 'Favorite', and Gilette, who was responsible for 'Caprice.' Today these models are regarded as of only mediocre quality, not in the modelling of the heads but because of the mixture of porcelains used in their manufacture and a certain roughness in the finish.

Apart from their mass-produced models, S.F.B.J. made two rather curious dolls around this time, 'Poulbot' and 'Poulbotte,' which were registered in France under their trademark in 1913, and which corresponded to series No. 239. They represented two typically French children, with red-blond hair, bright eyes, and appealing little faces. They were the work of the designer Francisque Poulbot (1879–1946), whose name and trademark were stamped on the nape of the necks. They too are great rarities today.

It is in fact extremely difficult now to find examples of these artist-designed dolls, especially those produced between the turn of the century and the First World War, and this has inevitably led to speculation about their success at the time they were made and the extent of their distribution compared with that of contemporary mass-produced models. It is clear that they were aimed at the most discriminating end of the market and that they were of superlative quality, succeeding as perhaps few others have done in the doll's original aim of representing the human being.

THE DOLLS

Preceding pages:

Wooden dolls

second half of the eighteenth century

54 cm (21¼ in.) and 50 cm (19½ in.)

A pair of beautiful dolls made entirely in wood. The features are sculpted and painted, and the articulated bodies represent adult women.

From the fact that they were sold at the Venice antiques market, and from information provided by their owners, it seems likely that they were manikin dolls made to promote the latest fashion at the Festa della Sensa in Venice. The clothes they are wearing are unfortunately not original, but antique materials have been used to make outfits in the style of the day.
Colombo collection.

Wooden doll

Germany(?), c. 1810

44 cm (17⅜ in.)

This wooden doll has sculpted and painted features and hair, and its body is articulated by means of pivots. The shoes are low and painted. The hairstyle and elongated lines of the figure are typically Napoleonic, and the clothes are original.
Fiamma and Laura Zanverdiani collection, Venice.

Wooden doll

Val Gardena, c. 1845

43 cm (17 in.)

Made entirely in wood, the body is adult and is articulated by means of ball and pivot joints. The features are sculpted and painted. The long earrings are also made of wood. Patrizia Bonato collection, Venice.

Doll with wooden head (background)
Germany or Austria, 1840–60
88 cm (34⅝ in.)

Wood was the principal material used by craftsmen and carvers in the construction of dolls and other toys from the earliest times. This model has all the characteristics of a Middle European doll of its period. Made at Sonneberg and Oberammergau, examples of this type were exported in large quantities to the rest of Europe. This one has its hair done in the classical style, with a chignon on the nape of the neck, which was fashionable at the time. The body is made of cotton with red stitching; the clothes are not original.
Private collection.

Doll with wooden head (left foreground)
Germany or Austria, 1840–60
45 cm (17⅝ in.)

Very similar to the doll above, this one has suffered damage to its face, which was originally painted. It was rediscovered in a Venetian attic with scraps of material that have been used to make it a new outfit in the style of the day.
Private collection.

Doll with wooden head (right foreground)
Val Gardena, 1845–50
43 cm (17 in.)

The head is made of wood, the body of stiff cloth, and the hands of kid. The clothes are all original and include two petticoats—one of piquet and one of batiste—and a jacket and skirt in printed cottons.
Mario Guadagnino collection, Venice.

Doll with papier-mâché head

Germany, 1830–40

50 cm ($19\frac{1}{2}$ in.)

The head and shoulders are modelled in one piece; the hair is painted black and the eyes brown; the mouth is closed. The body is made of stuffed cotton and the hands of hide. This doll was probably made at Sonneberg and advertised in a toy catalogue in Switzerland (see D.S., E.A. and E.J. Coleman, The Collector's Encyclopedia of Dolls, *p. 145); it was exported to France, from where it derives the name 'Pauline.' The clothes are not original.*
Private collection.

Doll with papier-mâché head

Germany, c. 1840

44 cm (17⅜ in.)

*This doll, which comes from the
House of Borromeo, has a well-made
head, the hair and face modelled and
painted in the style of the period. The
body is made of white kid. The
original evening gown is complete
with train.*
Borromeo collection, Isola Madre.

Doll with papier-mâché and wax head

Germany, second half of the nineteenth century

45 cm ($17\frac{5}{8}$ in.)

The head and shoulders are made in one piece, with a wax-coated Pompadour hairstyle, fixed glass eyes with black pupils, a cotton fabric body, and wooden arms and legs. The dress is not original. Private collection.

Papier-mâché and wax doll

Germany, 1840–45

40 cm ($15\frac{5}{8}$ in.)

The head is made of wax-coated papier-mâché, the glass eyes are fixed, and the body is white fabric with forearms of blue kid to simulate gloves. The hair is mohair and the outfit is entirely original.
Patrizia Bonato collection, Venice.

Small boy in papier-mâché and wax
Sonneberg, Germany, second half of
the nineteenth century
44 cm (17$\frac{3}{8}$ in.)

This doll shares some of the
characteristics of the Motschmann
type (articulation of the wrists and a
bellows mechanism for the voice, for
example), which were also produced
at Sonneberg. The head is made of
wax-covered papier-mâché, the fixed
eyes are of cobalt-blue glass, the body
is fabric, and the legs are wood, with
blue-painted boots with yellow
buttons. The outfit is original.
Patrizia Bonato collection, Venice.

'Bonnet doll'
Germany, c. 1860
56 cm (22 in.)

The head is made of wax-covered
composition, the body of fabric, and
the arms and legs of wood. The green
hat, which is made in one piece with
the head, is decorated with two red
feathers and a dark-blue ribbon. The
clothes are original.
Patrizia Bonato collection, Venice.

Doll with papier-mâché and wax
head of the Motschmann type
Germany, c. 1860
30 cm (11¾ in.)

The fixed eyes are of blue glass, the
lips are parted to show two teeth,
and the body is made of fabric and
composition, with the usual
articulation at ankle and wrist. The
stomach contains bellows for the
voice. The outfit is original.
Private collection.

Doll with wax-covered papier-mâché
head of the Motschmann type
Germany, second half of the
nineteenth century
42 cm (16½ in.)

The head has modelled hair and a
black-painted Alice band, mobile blue
glass eyes and parted lips showing
two teeth; the body is made of
cotton and the arms and legs of
composition, with articulation
at ankle and wrist. The voice
mechanism is operated by two cords.
The outfit is original.
Borromeo collection, Isola Madre.

Doll with wax-covered papier-mâché
head of the Motschmann type
Germany, second half of the
nineteenth century
57 cm (22⅜ in.)

The mobile eyes are made of cobalt-
blue glass, the lips are parted, and
the body is cotton with limbs of
composition, articulated at wrist and
ankle. The chest contains a voice
mechanism worked by cords. The
dress is partly original.
Borromeo collection, Isola Madre.

Black baby doll in wax

England, c. 1850–60

45 cm (17⅝ in.)

A baby doll with a wax head, fixed black glass eyes, a black fabric body, and wax limbs. It is striking not just for its pitch-blackness but particularly for the modelling of the head: its expression is entirely different from that of contemporaneous white dolls. Patrizia Bonato collection, Venice.

Doll with wax head

Montanari(?), England, second half of
the nineteenth century

53 cm (20$\frac{7}{8}$ in.)

The fixed eyes are grey glass, the
body is cotton, and the arms and legs
are wax. The outfit is original.
Borromeo collection, Isola Madre.

Doll with wax head

England, second half of the

nineteenth century

62 cm (24$\frac{1}{2}$ in.)

The head and shoulders are made of wax and the fixed eyes of blue glass; the mouth is closed, and the hair has been sewn into the scalp in little clumps. The body is cotton, with wax arms and legs. The outfit is original.
Borromeo collection, Isola Madre.

Doll with two faces, the head made
of wax-covered papier-mâché
F. Bartenstein, Germany, second half
of the nineteenth century
41 cm (16⅛ in.)

The faces, both with fixed brown
glass eyes, have two different
expressions, one crying, with the
mouth open and the tongue showing,
the other smiling, with the lips parted
to show a row of teeth. The head
turns on a pivot operated by a fine
cord, which at the same time works
the voice mechanism that makes a
little whimper. Another cord works
the arms and a third makes the doll
cry with long, loud sobs. The body
is made of cotton and stamped
'U.S.P.N. 243–702,' and the arms and
legs are composition. The clothes are
original.
Borromeo collection, Isola Madre.

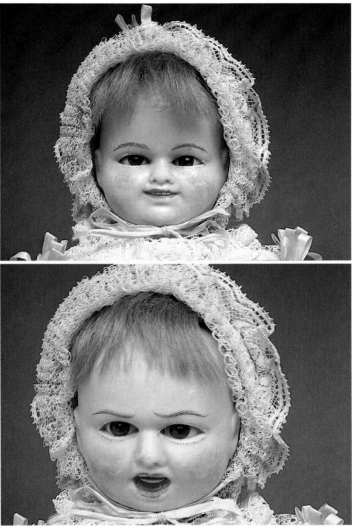

Doll with wax-covered papier-mâché
head
Germany, c. 1865
45 cm (17⅝ in.)

The head has the features of an
adult, with mobile eyes of blue glass
and pierced ears with earrings. The
body is made of fine cloth and
stuffed, and the limbs are papier-
mâché and wax. The short boots are
modelled in one piece with the feet.
The clothes are original.
Private collection.

Mechanical doll

Jules-Nicolas Steiner, France, 1855–60

40 cm ($15\frac{5}{8}$ in.)

This is one of the earliest of the Steiner dolls, with a head of wax-covered composition, fixed eyes of cobalt-blue glass, and lips parted to show rather crude bamboo teeth. The exaggerated modelling of the arms and legs is quite different from that of later types, and the limbs have no wax coating. The mechanism that allows it to perform the normal movements bears the trademark 'Steiner—Paris.' The clothes are original.
Private collection.

Doll with wax-covered papier-mâché head

Germany, c. 1880

37 cm (14½ in.)

A rather strange doll, with mobile brown eyes and a closed mouth. The body is made of composition and articulated at the ankle as well as the other main joints. The clothes are entirely original.
Borromeo collection, Isola Madre.

Preceding pages:

Doll with glazed porcelain head (far left)
Germany, 1845–50
33 cm (13 in.)

The head has painted features and modelled hair in the style known by collectors as the 'Covered Wagon.' The body is made of cotton with porcelain arms. The outfit is original.
Private collection.

Doll with porcelain head (below left)
Germany, c. 1850
28 cm (11 in.)

The head has painted features and black modelled hair. The body is cotton and the arms and legs are porcelain. The underwear is original but the dress is reproduction.
Private collection.

Doll with porcelain head (above centre)
Germany, c. 1840–45
85 cm (33¼ in.)

The style of the modelled hair suggests this dating. The body is made of white kid; the unusually well-finished hands have separated fingers. The boots and the underwear are original, but the rest of the outfit is reproduction.
Private collection.

Doll with glazed porcelain head (centre)
Germany, c. 1845
43 cm (17 in.)

Hair modelled in the style of the period has given this doll the name 'Flat Top.' The head has painted features and the body is cotton. The clothes are original.
Private collection.

Doll with glazed porcelain head (below centre)
Germany, c. 1850
21 cm (8⅜ in.)

The striking characteristic of this doll is that the modelled hair is blonde instead of the usual black. The body is cotton, with arms and legs in porcelain, the feet in delicately painted pink boots. The underwear is original.
Private collection.

Doll with glazed porcelain head (right)
Schlaggenwald (1793–1925), Bohemia, c. 1845
40 cm (15⅝ in.)

The features are painted and the porcelain has been tinted a delicate pink. The rounded head has part of the scalp blackened by the glue used to attach the hair. The clothes are not original.
Private collection.

Doll in glazed porcelain (page 137)

Germany, 1840–50

26 cm (10¼ in.)

This delightful little doll has survived intact, still in the box in which it was sent to the purchaser. It has painted features and modelled hair; the body is made of fabric and the arms of leather. It has various items of underwear and changes of clothes, all of them completely original.
Patrizia Bonato collection, Venice.

The oyster seller

Germany, 1840–50

15 cm (6 in.)

The head in glazed porcelain has modelled hair and painted features; there are earrings in the pierced ears; the limbs are made of bisque and the body of stuffed fabric. The unusual woollen dress is decorated with shells, and hanging from the belt is an oyster shell 'basket' and a knife to open the oysters.
Private collection.

Head in glazed porcelain

Germany, c. 1860

14 cm (5$\frac{1}{2}$ in.)

This superb example of an adult female head has finely modelled hair decorated with painted flowers. The porcelain of the face is delicately tinted and the features are painted with great artistry.
Patrizia Bonato collection, Venice.

Doll in glazed porcelain

Germany, 1840–45

26 cm ($10\frac{1}{4}$ in.)

The head has modelled and painted face and hair; the body is wood articulated by means of pivots; the arms and legs are porcelain with painted stockings and shoes. The dress is original.
Private collection.

'Jenny Lind' doll

Germany, 1850–60

50 cm (19½ in.)

The features and hairstyle of the glazed porcelain head were inspired by the famous Swedish soprano Jenny Lind (1820–1887). The rather rudimentary body is made of cotton with forearms in kid. The dress is reproduction.
Patrizia Bonato collection, Venice.

Doll in glazed porcelain

Germany, 1860

57 cm (22$\frac{3}{8}$ in.)

The rounded head has painted features and real hair done in an elaborate style and decorated with a brass comb. The body is made of stuffed fabric and the arms and legs of porcelain, with modelled and painted shoes. Both the velvet dress and the underwear are original. Private collection.

Doll with Alice band

Germany, c. 1860

The head is modelled in glazed porcelain, with painted chestnut hair and a gold-and-white Alice band. The arms and legs and little black boots are also porcelain. The head turns on a pivot, and the Motschmann-type body in fabric and papier-mâché has a bellows voice system. The outfit is original.
Patrizia Bonato collection, Venice.

Group of dolls in glazed porcelain
Germany, 1850–1914
From 5 cm to 37 cm (2 in. to 14½ in.)

*These are known as 'bath dolls'
because they could be bathed without
damaging them. They are also known
as 'frozen Charlies'. They were made
in Germany, either in glazed
porcelain or bisque, with modelled or
painted hair, the skin coloured all
over, sometimes black, or just the
face tinted, with rosy cheeks. They
generally represent standing babies,
the hands closed in a fist, and they
have no articulation.
Private collection.*

Parian doll with bisque head

Germany, 1850–80

70 cm (27½ in.)

Dolls with sculpted blonde hair, painted features, and pale faces with rosy cheeks are known as 'Parian.' The name derives from the marble of the Greek island of Paros, which is noted for its whiteness. This is a particularly large and splendid example, modelled and painted with great skill and delicacy. It has pierced ears, a closed mouth, and fair hair held back by a blue ribbon. The body is made of kid and the arms of composition. The dress is not original.
Private collection.

Preceding pages:

Triplets with bisque heads
_____
Germany, c. 1860
_____
30 cm (11¾ in.)
_____

Similar to the doll described on page
152, these triplets combine glazed
porcelain hair with bisque faces and
shoulders; the features are sculpted
and painted. Their backs are marked
'1064,' which may denote 'Sitsendorf.'
They are almost identical; the only
real difference is the colour of the
hair: one blonde, one dark, one
brunette. The bodies are made of
cotton and two of them have arms
and legs of bisque, while the third
has arms of leather. The dresses are
original.
Private collection.

'Empress Eugénie' doll
_____
Germany, 1865–70
_____
53 cm (20⅞ in.)
_____

Throughout the nineteenth century,
fashions were set by women in public
life, some of whom as a result
became ideals of style and beauty.
One such was the Empress Eugénie of
France, portrayed here in one of her
famous head-dresses. The modelling
and painting of this bisque head are
of exceptionally high quality, the
head-dress itself glazed in irridescent
violet, gold, and white. The body is
made of cotton with arms of leather.
The boned corset, the dress, and
some of the underwear are original.
Private collection.

Parian doll with bisque head

Germany, second half of the

nineteenth century

42 cm (16½ in.)

Unlike many of the dolls on the preceding pages, the delicately made head of this doll has fixed eyes of blue glass. The blonde hair is modelled and painted. The body is made of cotton, with arms and legs in bisque; on its feet are boots painted in irridescent pink. The dress is original.
Colombo collection.

'Alice' doll with bisque head

Germany, second half of the

nineteenth century

23 cm (9 in.)

Inspired by Lewis Carroll's Alice, this doll has modelled and painted features and hair and wears a black Alice band. Its body is made of cotton with limbs in bisque, the shoes painted irridescent gold. The dress and underwear are entirely original. Private collection.

Doll with bisque head

Germany, c. 1900

33 cm (13 in.)

Made in white bisque, and also in other materials, dolls such as these were produced from 1860 until 1916 in France, Germany, and even Japan. This one wears a hat that was in fashion around the turn of the century. The body is made of fabric and the limbs of bisque. The dress is not original.
Private collection.

Preceding pages:

Manikin doll with bisque head

E. Barrois, France, 1860–65

53 cm (20⅞ in.)

One of the earliest French doll factories was owned by Mme Barrois and was based in the Rue St Martin, Paris. This example of her work has fixed blue eyes, a closed mouth, and pierced ears. It is marked 'E.6 B.' The body is made in white kid and has no articulation at the neck. The dress is contemporaneous but in fact belongs to another doll, in the Levi-Morenos collection in Venice.
Private collection.

Manikin doll

Blampoix Senior, France, 1860–70

47 cm (18½ in.)

The head is bisque, with articulation at the neck, fixed eyes of blue glass, a closed mouth, and pierced ears. The back is marked 'B-S.' The body is made of kid and contains a voice mechanism operated by two cords. The dress, which is not original, is a little later in style than the doll itself. Private collection.

Manikin doll

France, c. 1860

47 cm (18½ in.)

The head and shoulders are bisque,
without articulation at the neck; the
eyes are fixed blue glass; the mouth is
closed; the body is kid with bisque
arms. The check dress of silk taffeta
and the blouse beneath of fine,
tucked cotton are both original.
Patrizia Bonato collection, Venice.

Manikin doll

France, 1860–65

40 cm (15⅝ in.)

The head and sholders are bisque, with fixed blue eyes and pierced ears; the body is kid, with gussets for movement and bisque arms. The silk faille walking dress has a short jacket and a full tiered skirt with a short train; the outfit is entirely original. Patrizia Bonato collection, Venice.

Manikin doll with bisque head

France, c. 1875

44 cm ($17\frac{3}{8}$ in.)

Probably attributable to François Gaultier, this doll has head and shoulders of bisque, fixed eyes of grey glass, and a body of kid, with gussets for movement. The 'polonaise' walking dress is made of spotted grosgrain silk in ivory with brown sleeves and is trimmed with brown tassels and bows. The outfit, including the matching hat, is entirely original.
Private collection.

Manikin doll with bisque head

François Gaultier, France, c. 1870

*The head and shoulders are bisque
and the eyes are blue glass; the back
is marked 'F.G.' The body is made
of kid, with gussets for movement.
This manikin doll wears a summer
walking dress in pink and white
striped cotton with buttons down the
front and a short train at the back.
The outfit is entirely original.
Private collection.*

Manikin doll

Jumeau, France, c. 1880

37 cm (14½ in.)

The bisque head has articulation at the neck, fixed eyes of blue glass, closed mouth, and pierced ears. The nape of the neck is marked '4' and shows traces of a red die-stamp. The body is made of white kid, and the outfit is reproduction.
Private collection.

Preceding pages:

Manikin doll with wardrobe

France, 1865–70

58 cm (22¾ in.)

The head and shoulders are pale bisque; the neck is articulated and marked with an etched figure 5 and two vertical bars. The body is made entirely of wood and articulated by means of pivots at the ankles, wrists, and waist. Its construction is similar to a doll made by Léon-Casimir Bru and patented in 1869.

    This manikin still has part of its elaborate wardrobe, including elegant walking and day dresses and fine underwear. Embroidered on its nightdress and dressing gown are the initials 'M.C.' surmounted by a crown; it is thought that the doll originally belonged to the House of Savoy.
Borromeo collection, Isola Madre.

Doll with bisque head

Germany, 1880–90

65 cm (25⅝ in.)

The head and shoulders are in one piece, without articulation at the neck, and the blue-grey eyes are mobile. Marked with an 'O' on the back, the body is made of leather with seams stitched in red, and the arms are bisque. The dress is partially original.
Borromeo collection, Isola Madre.

Mechanical doll

Jules-Nicolas Steiner, France, 1867

52 cm (20½ in.)

The rounded head is high-quality bisque with fixed eyes of blue glass and lips parted to reveal two rows of teeth. The cardboard body contains a spring mechanism that allows the doll to move and cry. The arms and legs are composition covered with a fine layer of wax. A label on the stomach, under the leather that hides the internal workings, reads: 'Livré le 0/10.1867—M. Verret de Vienne—J.N. Steiner fabricant, rue de Saintonge, N.25, à Paris—Prissette. Imp. Pass. du Caire, 17.' The outfit is not original.
Private collection.

Doll with bisque head of the 'Belton'
type

Germany, second half of the
nineteenth century

40 cm ($15\frac{5}{8}$ in.)

This definition generally refers to a doll with a rounded bisque head, linked to the body by means of one or more holes in the top. It was produced around the mid-nineteenth century by a number of German firms, and was also exported to France. The name 'Belton' derives from P.F. Jumeau's associate, who used this type of head for the dolls he assembled in Paris. Very few round-headed dolls of this type were made by French manufacturers, not even by Jumeau, which conflicts with the view mistakenly held by many collectors.

This doll was probably made by the German firm of Baehr & Proeschild, and has a closed mouth, fixed brown eyes, and a body of composition and wood with articulation by means of ball joints. It was rediscovered with the dress it wears in the photograph.
Private collection.

Doll with bisque head

François Gaultier, France, c. 1880

25 cm (9¾ in.)

The head and shoulders are bisque, with an articulated neck. The doll has fixed eyes of grey glass, a closed mouth, and pierced ears. The body is made of leather, with gussets for movement and forearms of bisque. It is marked 'F.1G.' on the back and on the head.
Patrizia Bonato collection, Venice.

Doll with bisque head

François Gaultier, France, c. 1880

53 cm (20⅞ in.)

This is a top-quality head, with fixed blue eyes, a closed mouth, and pierced ears. It is marked on the nape of the neck with the etched stamp 'F.9 G.' The body is made of composition and wood, with articulation by means of ball joints. The underwear is original and the dress reproduction.
Private collection.

Doll with bisque head

Jules-Nicolas Steiner, France,

c. *1870–75*

40 cm ($15\frac{5}{8}$ in.)

Head in very pale—almost white—bisque, with fixed grey glass eyes, pierced ears, and an open mouth showing two rows of teeth. The head is unstamped but 'Steiner-Paris' appears on the voice mechanism. The body is composition and wood, with ball-joint articulation. The underwear is original and the dress reproduction. Private collection.

Mechanical doll

Jules-Nicolas Steiner, France, c. 1875

45 cm (17⅝ in.)

An example of the famous 'automatic speaking doll' patented in 1862, this doll has a rounded head in pale bisque with fixed glass eyes, pierced ears, and an open mouth showing two rows of teeth. The arms and legs are in papier-mâché covered with wax; the torso is cardboard and contains a spring mechanism allowing the doll to turn its head, move its limbs, and cry 'Mama' and 'Papa.' The doll is seen here with its extensive original wardrobe. Patrizia Bonato collection, Venice.

Doll with bisque head

Jules-Nicolas Steiner, c. 1885

60 cm ($23\frac{5}{8}$ in.)

The head has mobile eyes operated by a lever, a closed mouth, and pierced ears. It is stamped on the nape of the neck 'St.C 1.' The articulated body is made of composition and cardboard. The dress and underwear are original. Private collection.

Preceding pages:

Doll with bisque head
Jules-Nicolas Steiner, France, c. 1889
53 cm (20⅞ in.)

The mobile blue eyes are operated by a lever (marked 'Steiner'); the lips are parted to show two rows of teeth; the ears are delicately modelled and pierced. On the nape of the neck is the etched mark. 'Figure B n. 3—J. Steiner Bte S.G.D.G.—Paris,' and the papier-mâché skull is marked '3.' The articulated body is made of composition and contains a voice mechanism—labelled: 'Le Petit Parisien–Bébé J. Steiner–Marque Déposé–Medaille d'Or Paris 1889'— which enables the doll to say 'Papa' and 'Mama.' The hands are particularly finely modelled, and the articulated wrists are marked with an etched figure 3 to indicate the size. The outfit, underwear, and mohair wig are all original.
Private collection.

Doll with bisque head
Jules-Nicolas Steiner, c. 1890
62 cm (24½ in.)

The blue eyes are fixed, the mouth is closed, and the ears are pierced; the nape of the neck is etched with the company's trademark, 'J.N. Steiner— Fre, A-Paris.' The articulated body is made of composition. The dress is partially original.
Mᵉ Rossi collection.

'My dream baby' doll
Armand Marseille, Germany, c. 1924
35 cm (13¾ in.)

The rounded bisque head has mobile eyes and an open mouth showing the tongue; the body is light fabric and the hands composition. The doll is marked with the series number and designer's initials, '351—A.M.' The outfit and pram are original.
Private collection.

Doll with bisque head

Jumeau(?), France, 1876–80

45 cm ($17\frac{5}{8}$ in.)

_The face of this doll, absolutely
unique of its type, is painted with the
minutest attention to detail, the
contours and features defined with
great care and subtlety. The eyes are
grey-blue glass, the mouth is half
open, and the ears are pierced. The
body, articulated by means of
wooden ball-joints, is made of
composition and wood. It has no
marks whatever to help us identify its
maker, but it seems likely to have
been Jumeau. Generally speaking,
models of this sort are known as
'portrait' dolls, but in the light of
recent research this definition seems
inappropriate; a more accurate
classification would be simply 'Bébé
Incassable,' or boxed doll, examples
of which were made between about
1876 and 1884, before the classic
'Bébé Jumeau' model appeared. The
outfit is original._
Private collection.

Doll with bisque head

Jumeau, France, 1879–80

68 cm (26¾ in.)

This is a very beautiful example of a doll from the early days of Jumeau production, with well-defined and expressive features. It has a closed mouth, fixed hazel-brown glass eyes, and pierced ears. The nape of the neck is marked '12 X.' The body is made of wood and composition and articulated by eight ball-joints. A blue die-stamp on the back reads 'Jumeau Medaille d'Or-Paris.' The dress and underwear are all original.
Private collection.

Doll with bisque head

Jumeau, France, c. 1885

56 cm (22 in.)

The head has closed mouth, fixed eyes in hazel-coloured glass, and pierced ears. The nape of the neck bears the engraved mark 'Déposé E 10 J.' The articulated body in composition and wood has a blue stamp on the back: 'Jumeau Medaille d'Or-Paris.' The dress, hat, and underwear are original. The trunk spills over with other clothes and accessories of the period, including some paper doll costumes.
Private collection.

Mechanical doll with bisque head:

'L'Intrépide Bebe'

France, c. 1893

45 cm (17⅝ in.)

Patented in 1893 by the firm of Roullet & Decamps, which specialized in mechanical and automatic dolls, this model walks by means of a clockwork mechanism that allows it to raise and lower its legs. The beautiful head was made by Jumeau and has fixed blue eyes, typically well-defined eyebrows, and a closed mouth. It is marked 'L'Intrépide—R.D.—B.S.G.D.G 7—Déposé' and 'R.D.'—the initials of the firm. The dress is reproduction but the shoes, bearing the trademark design of a bee, are original. Private collection.

Doll with bisque head
Bébé Jumeau, France, c. 1890
38 cm (15 in.)

*The head has an open mouth and
fixed blue eyes; the nape of the neck
is marked with the red stamp
'Déposé-Tête Jumeau' and an etched
figure 5. The articulated body is
made of composition and wood and
stamped 'Bébé Jumeau Bte S.G.D.G.
Déposé.' The hair, earrings, shoes,
and smock dress are all original.
Patrizia Bonato collection, Venice.*

Bébé caractère
S.F.B.J., France, c. 1910
39 cm (15⅜ in.)

*The rounded head is modelled in
bisque, with fixed blue glass eyes, a
half-open smiling mouth, and a body
of composition and papier-mâché
with rigid legs and articulated arms.
It was one of the greatest successes of
the S.F.B.J., whose initials are
marked on the nape of the neck,
along with '226—Paris.' The outfit is
not original.
Patrizia Bonato collection, Venice.*

Preceding pages:

Doll with bisque head

Paris Bébé—Danel & Cie, France,

c. 1890

55 cm (21⅝ in.)

The head has a closed mouth, fixed blue eyes, and pierced ears; on the nape of the neck is the etched stamp 'Paris Bébé—Tête Déposé 9.' The articulated body made of composition and wood is marked with a stamp of the Eiffel Tower. The firm of Danel & Cie registered the trademark 'Paris Bébé' when they started the business; in 1896 they were absorbed by Jumeau. The outfit is original. Patrizia Bonato collection, Venice.

Doll with bisque head

Rabery & Delphieu, France, c. 1890

35 cm (13¾ in.)

The head has fixed brown eyes, a closed mouth, and pierced ears. The etched mark on the nape of the neck reads 'R. 4/O D.' The body is made of composition and wood and is stamped on the back 'Bébé Rabery-Paris.' The dress, hair, and accessories are all original. Private collection.

Doll with bisque head

Jullien, France, 1885–90

70 cm ($27\frac{1}{2}$ in.)

The head has fixed blue glass eyes, a closed mouth, and pierced ears. 'Paris' is etched on the nape of the neck. The articulated body is made of composition and wood. On the soles of the shoes is the mark 'J. Jne.' The outfit is contemporary with the doll. Elio Filoni collection, Milan.

Doll with bisque head

Léon-Casimir Bru, France, c. 1880

85 cm (33½ in.)

This is an important example of the Bébé Bru, with a leather body of the early type and a head with fixed blue glass eyes, a half-open mouth, and pierced ears. It bears an etched stamp on the nape of the neck, 'Bru Jne 11.' The arms are made of bisque. The dress is not original.
Borromeo collection, Isola Madre.

Doll with bisque head

Bébé Jumeau, France, c. 1880

73 cm (28⅝ in.)

The head has a closed mouth and fixed blue eyes, the ears are attached separately. A red die-stamp on the nape of the neck reads 'Déposé-Tête Jumeau 13,' the number etched. The body, made of wood and composition, is articulated and marked 'Bebe Jumeau Bte S.G.D.G. Déposé.' The dress is original and bears the label 'Maison Parisienne Bertone & C. Milano.'
Patrizia Bonato collection, Venice.

Doll with bisque head

Léon-Casimir Bru, France, c. 1885

61 cm (24 in.)

This doll is a beautiful example of the traditional Bébé Bru, with fixed hazel eyes, a closed mouth, and pierced ears. It is marked on the nape of the neck 'Bru Jne 9,' and the same mark appears on the bisque shoulders. The body is made of kid (the H. Chevrot model, patented in 1883), and bears a trademark and the blue die-stamp 'Bébé-Bru.' The arms are bisque and the legs wooden. The outfit is antique but not contemporary, but the shoes are original and are marked on the sole 'Bébé Bru 9,' as are the boned corset and other underwear.
Private collection.

Doll with bisque head

Léon-Casimir Bru, France, c. 1880

33 cm (13 in.)

The head has fixed blue eyes, a closed mouth, and pierced ears; on the nape of the neck is the engraved stamp 'Bru Jne 2.' The articulated body is made of wood and composition. The outfit is not original.
Colombo collection.

Preceding pages:

Black baby doll (page 224)

Heubach Köppelsdorf

Germany, c. 1930

30 cm (11¾ in.)

The rounded bisque head has black eyes that move sideways, a smiling open mouth, pierced nostrils with a metal ring through them and pierced ears with hoop earrings. The body is made of composition and articulated, and it is marked on the neck 'Heuback–Köppelsdorf 463 11/0.'
Private collection.

Black baby doll (page 225 above left)

Heubach, Germany, c. 1920

21 cm (8⅜ in.)

The rounded head has modelled and painted features; the neck is marked with a daisy design and the reference '7671—0—Germany.' The body is composition.
Private collection.

Indian squaw (above left)

Armand Marseille, Germany, 1925–30

22 cm (8⅝ in.)

The bisque head has fixed black eyes and parted lips. The articulated body represents an adult and is made of composition. The outfit is original.
Private collection.

Mexican baby doll (above left)

Heubach Köppelsdorf, Germany,

1920–25

26 cm (10¼ in.)

The rounded head has mobile black glass eyes and an open mouth. The neck is marked 'Heubach-Köppelsdorf—452.14/0 Germany.' The articulated body is composition with rigid legs. The outfit is not original.
Private collection.

Mixed-race doll (above right)

France, c. 1900

35 cm (13¾ in.)

This doll, probably attributable to the Jumeau factory, has a bisque head with fixed brown eyes, an open mouth, and pierced ears. The articulated body is made of wood and composition, and the nape of the neck is etched 'X-3.' The dress is original.
Patrizia Bonato collection, Venice.

Doll with bisque head (above right)

Schoenau & Hoffmeister, Germany,

c. 1900

57 cm (22⅜ in.)

The doll has fixed brown eyes and an open mouth. On the nape of the neck is the mark 'SPB' in a Star of David, followed by 'H.' The body is made of composition and wood and the outfit is original.
Patrizia Bonato collection, Venice.

Pair of Oriental dolls (below left)

Germany, c. 1890–1910

32 cm (12⅝ in.)

These twins have fixed black glass eyes and closed mouths. The heads are made of papier-mâché, the body of fabric, and the limbs of composition. They are exceptionally finely modelled examples of this type of ethnic doll, complete with their original outfits.
Patrizia Bonato collection, Venice.

Oriental doll (below centre)

Kestner, Germany, c. 1910

45 cm (17⅝ in.)

The head has mobile brown eyes, an open mouth and Burmese characteristics. There is an etched mark on the nape of the neck: '25 164.' The body is made of composition and wood, articulated by means of ball joints. The kimono is original.
Private collection.

Oriental baby doll (below centre, foreground)

Armand Marseille, Germany, c. 1920

25 cm (9¾ in.)

The rounded head has mobile black eyes and a closed mouth. A mark on the nape of the neck reads 'A M. Germany—353/2/OK.' The body is made of composition, with rigid legs. The greenish tint of the skin is decidedly odd and casts serious doubts on the doll's ethnic origins. The outfit is reproduction.
Private collection.

Mixed race doll with bisque head (below right)

Jules-Nicolas Steiner, France, end of the nineteenth century

37 cm (14½ in.)

The head has fixed eyes of hazel-coloured glass, an open mouth, and pierced ears. The nape of the neck is stamped 'Le Parisien—S.G.D.G.—A 7.' The articulated body is made of composition, and the costume is original.
Borromeo collection, Isola Madre.

Good luck doll

E. Denamur, France, c. 1890

41 cm (16⅛ in.)

The bisque head has an open mouth and fixed eyes, with an etched mark on the nape of the neck, 'E 6 D—Déposé.' The body is made of composition with rigid limbs. The doll is dressed as a fortune-teller and the costume is original. Stitched beneath the skirt are a series of 'leaves' that open to reveal a printed message; they must be chosen with eyes closed in order to discover the secrets of the future.
Patrizia Bonato collection, Venice.

Walking doll

Simon & Halbig, Germany, 1900–10

35 cm (13¾ in.)

The bisque head has fixed pale blue eyes and an open mouth. The nape of the neck is marked 'S H 1079-DEP-Germany 4 1/2.' The body, with arms articulated at the wrist and rigid legs, is made of composition and contains a clockwork mechanism—probably made by Roullet & Decamps—which is operated by a key. The outfit is reproduction but the underwear is original.
Private collection.

Doll with bisque head

François Gaultier, France, c. 1900

56 cm (22 in.)

The head has fixed blue eyes, an open mouth, and pierced ears, and is marked with a scroll stamp and the initials 'F.G.' The body represents an adult and is made of wood and composition, with articulated arms and rigid legs. The magnificent wedding dress and the underwear beneath are all entirely original. M. Rossi collection.

Doll with bisque head
Kämmer & Reinhardt, Germany,
1905–10
43 cm (17 in.)

This is perhaps the most celebrated doll to have been produced by Kämmer & Reinhardt. It has a closed mouth and mobile blue glass eyes, and the nape of the neck is marked 'K [followed by a star] R-S & H— 117/A 43.' The body, which is made of composition and wood, is articulated by means of ball joints, and has a label on the back from the famous toyshop of Bonini in Turin, which was mentioned by Edmondo De Amicis in his book The King of the Dolls. *The dress is contemporary with the doll.*
Private collection.

Doll with bisque head

Furga, Italy, 1918–20

93 cm (36⅝ in.)

The head has mobile eyes of blue glass, an open mouth, and an etched mark on the nape of the neck that reads 'Furga Canneto S/Oglio 900.' The articulated body is made of composition and wood. The dress is contemporary with the doll.
Patrizia Bonato collection, Venice.

Clown

Furga, Italy, c. 1920

35 cm (13¾ in.)

The bisque head has fixed black eyes and a smiling, closed mouth. The nape of the neck bears the mark 'Furga Canneto S/Oglio.' The neck moves on a flange and the simple wooden body is articulated at the shoulders and hips. The outfit is reproduction.
Patrizia Bonato collection, Venice.

Bébé caractère

Furga, Italy, 1920–25

37 cm (14½ in.)

The rounded bisque head has mobile brown eyes and an open mouth showing two bottom teeth. The body is made of stuffed fabric with celluloid hands. It is marked on the nape of the neck 'Furga Canneto S/Oglio 4.' This high-quality doll was clearly modelled on others of the period but is superior to contemporary dolls of a similar type made by Furga. The dress is original.
Patrizia Bonato collection, Venice.

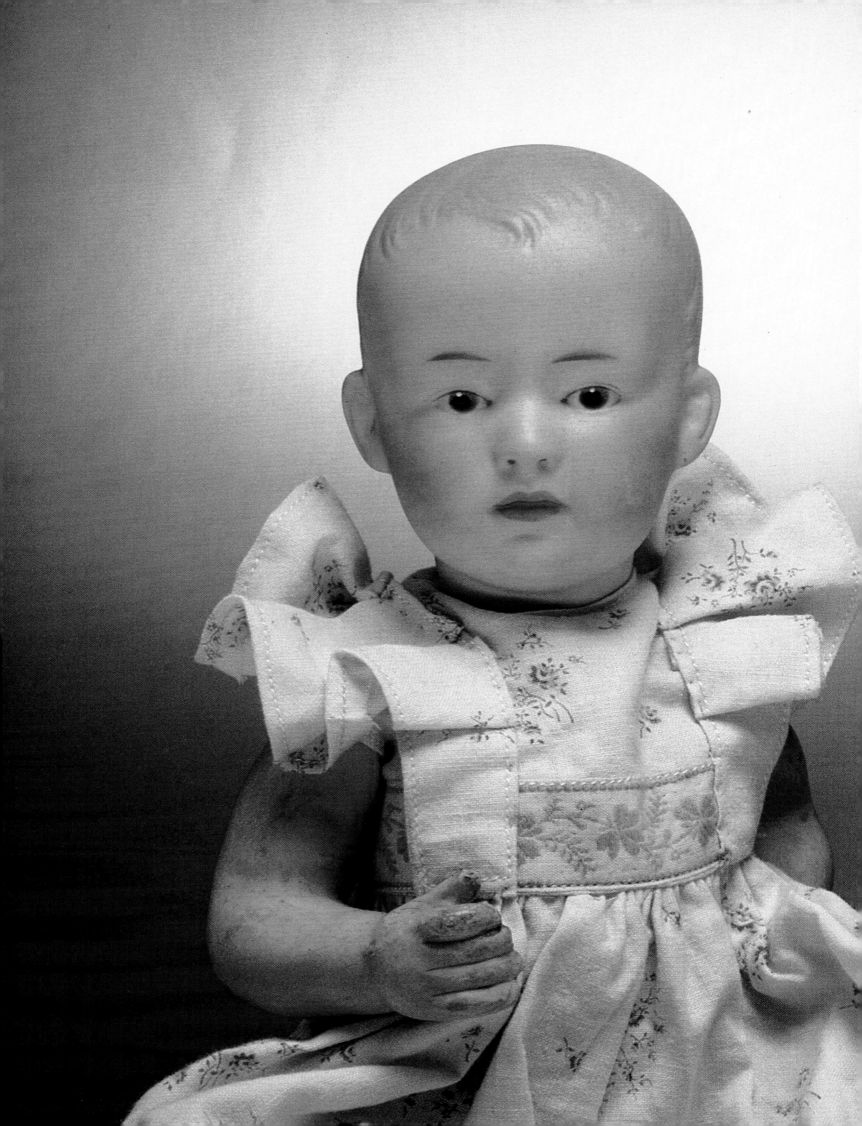

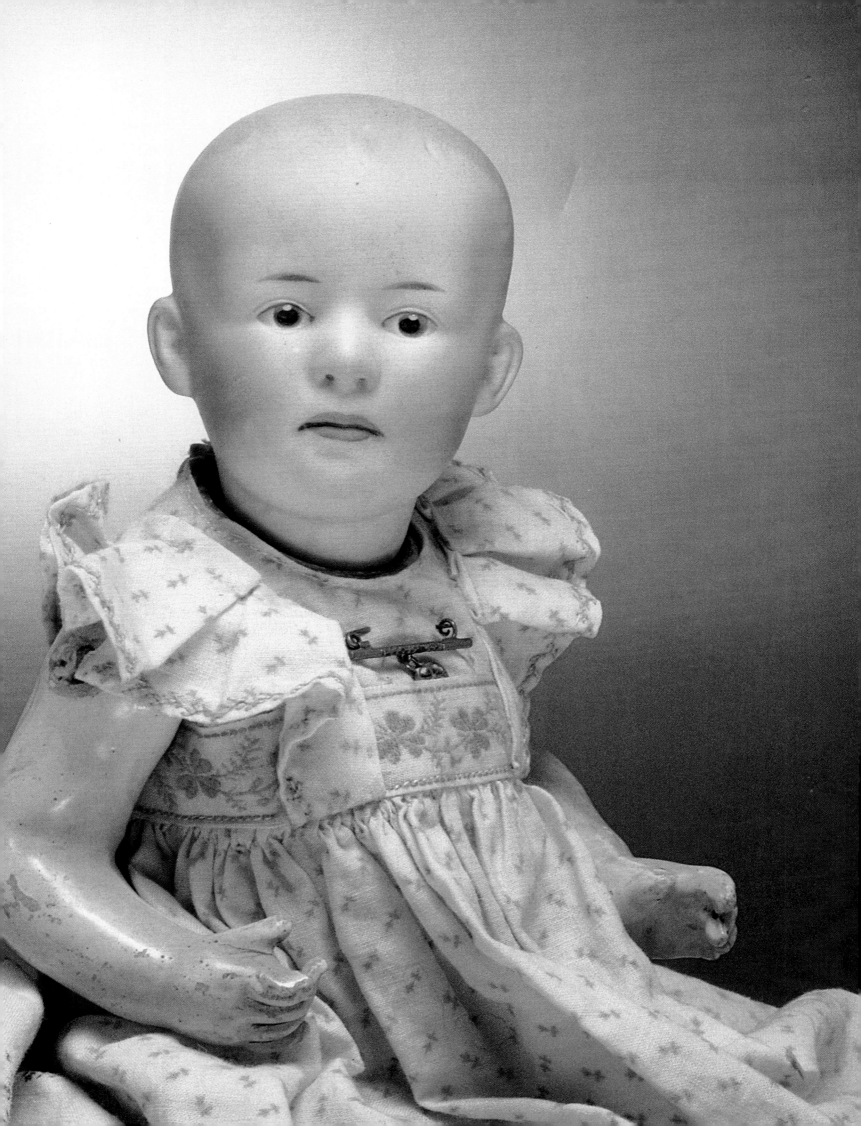

Bébé caractère (page 238)
Gebrüder Heubach, Germany, c. 1915
30 cm (11¾ in.)

The bisque head has modelled and painted eyes, and a closed mouth. The doll is marked with the serial number 7602. The articulated composition body represents a newborn baby. The dress is contemporary with the doll.
Patrizia Bonato collection, Venice.

Bébé caractère (page 239)
Gebrüder Heubach, Germany, c. 1915
30 cm (11¾ in.)

This doll is similar to the previous model, but with a different mouth and serial number—this one is marked 7603. The dress is original.
Patrizia Bonato collection, Venice.

Bébé caractère (preceding pages)
Kestner, Germany, c. 1900
26 cm (10¼ in.)

Made entirely in bisque, this doll has mobile eyes and a half-open mouth. The body is finely modelled and represents a newborn baby. It is marked 'J.D.K. 211.' The outfit is contemporary with the doll.
Patrizia Bonato collection, Venice.

'Coquette' (standing)
Gebrüder Heubach, Germany, c. 1912
20 cm (7⅞ in.)

This doll is made entirely in bisque with modelled and painted features, hair, socks, and shoes, and articulation at the shoulders and hips. The outfit is original.
Patrizia Bonato collection, Venice.

Bébé caractère: 'Stuart Baby' (seated)
Gebrüder Heubach, Germany, c. 1910
23 cm (9 in.)

Known as 'Stuart Babies' by collectors, 'caractère' dolls of this type have bonnets modelled in bisque with the head; this one wears a bonnet painted with a garland of flowers. The eyes are also painted, the mouth is closed, and the composition body represents a newborn baby. It is marked with the serial number 7977. The dress is contemporary with the doll.
Patrizia Bonato collection, Venice.

Bébé caractère with two faces

Kley & Hann, Germany, c. 1912

35 cm (13¾ in.)

The bisque head has two faces: one smiling, with mobile glass eyes and a half-open mouth showing modelled teeth, the other crying, with painted downcast eyes. The composition body represents a newborn baby. The dress is contemporary with the doll. Patrizia Bonato collection, Venice.

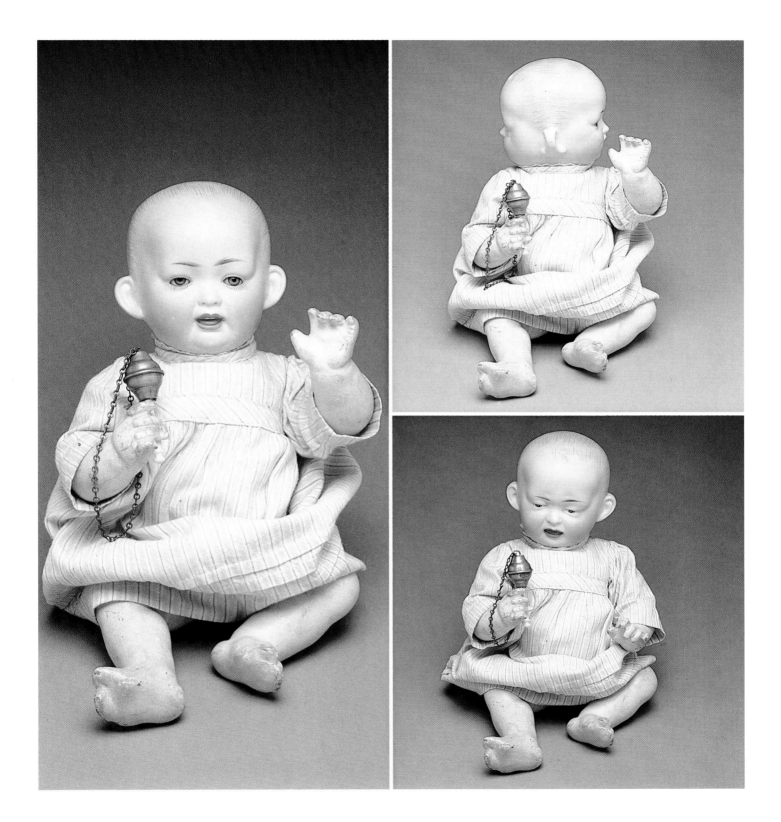

Bébé caractère

Kestner, Germany, 1910–20

34 cm (13$\frac{3}{8}$ in.)

The bisque head has mobile eyes looking to the side (known as 'flirting') and lips parted to show teeth and a tongue. The composition body represents a newborn baby and contains bellows for the voice. The nape of the neck is marked 'J.D.K. 257.' This was one of Kestner's most successful models. The outfit is contemporary with the doll. Patrizia Bonato collection, Venice.

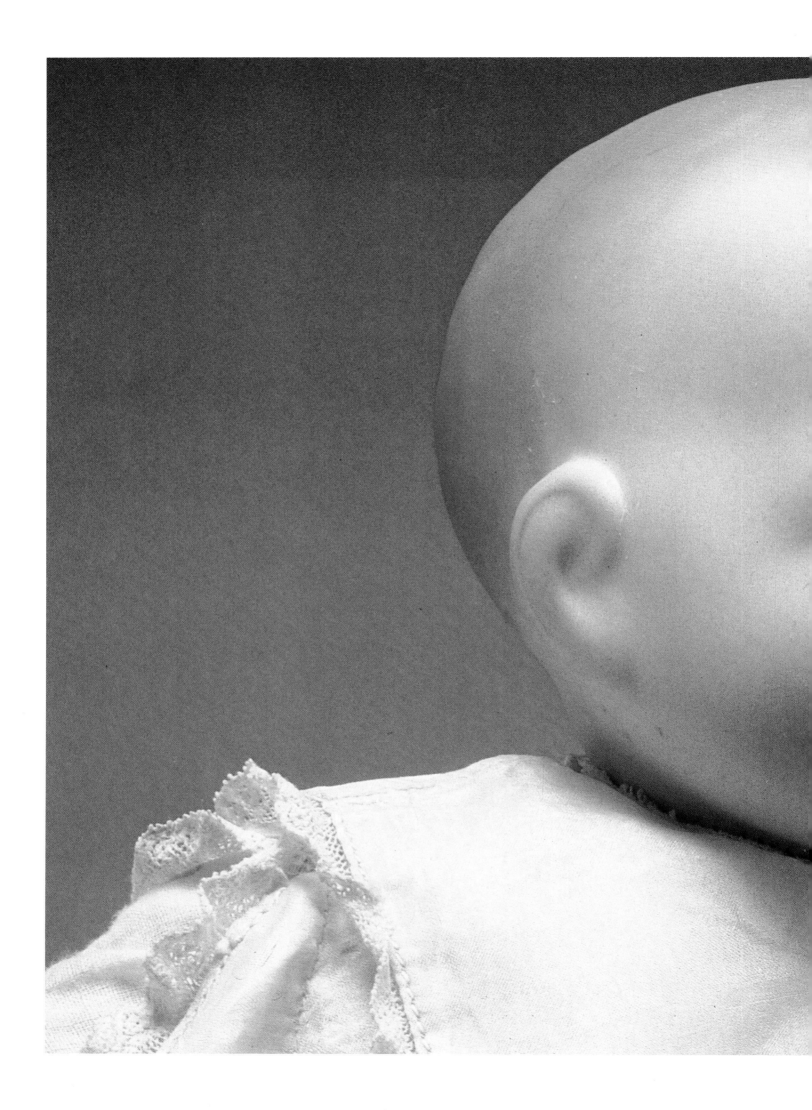

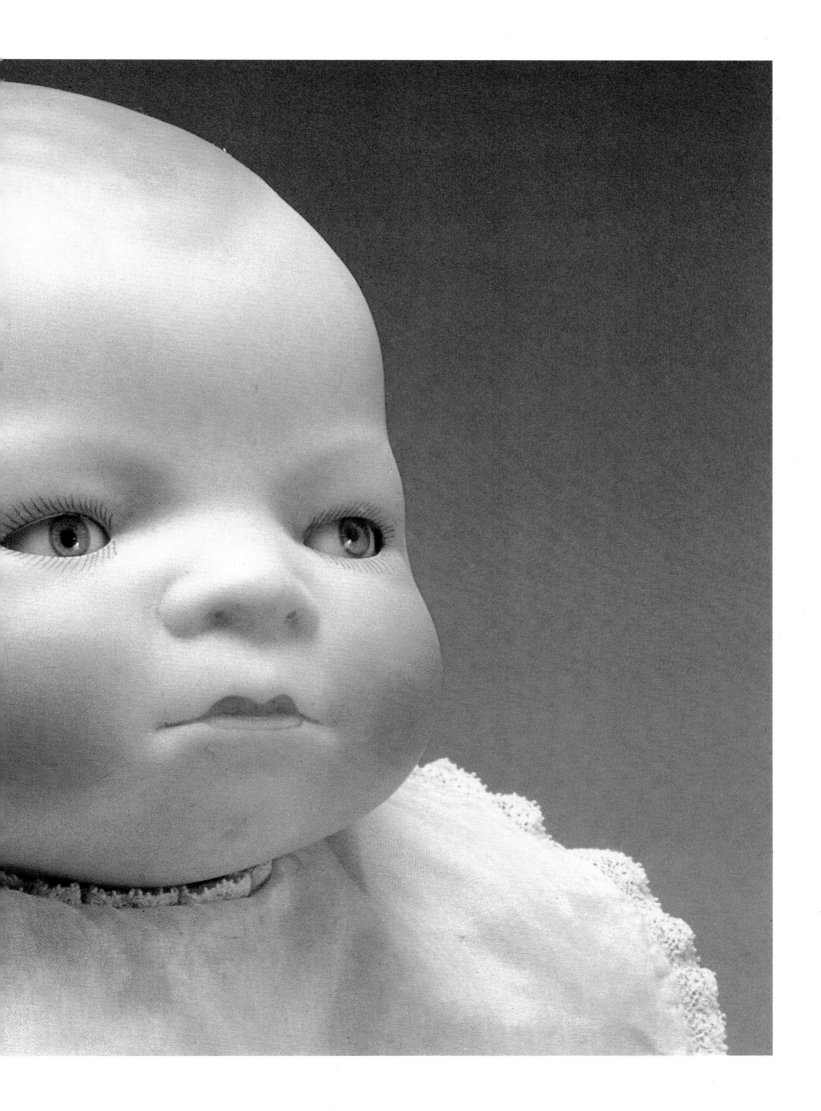

Preceding pages:

Bébé caractère

By-lo Baby, America, 1922–25

33 cm (13 in.)

The first in a long line of newborn baby dolls, this one is particularly remarkable for its realism. The rounded head is made of bisque with mobile blue glass eyes, and the hands are celluloid. The body, of pale pink fabric, contains a voice mechanism. On the nape of the neck is the etched mark 'Copy by Grace S. Putnam.' The dress is original.
Patrizia Bonato collection, Venice.

'Googlie' (seated)

Armand Marseille, Germany, 1920–25

30 cm (11¾ in.)

The bisque head has eyes looking to the side and a closed, smiling mouth. The nape of the neck is marked 'A.M. 323.' The body is made of composition with modelled shoes and socks. The outfit is contemporary with the doll.
Patrizia Bonato collection, Venice.

'Googlie' (standing)

Armand Marseille, Germany, 1920–25

35 cm (13¾ in.)

The bisque head has mobile eyes looking to the side and a closed, smiling mouth. The mark on the nape of the neck reads 'A.M. 323.' The body is made entirely of composition with rigid arms and legs. The outfit is contemporary with the doll.
Patrizia Bonato collection, Venice.

Bébé caractère

Armand Marseille, Germany, 1920–25

18 cm (7 in.)

The head in modelled bisque has painted eyes and a closed mouth. The body is made of composition with modelled shoes and socks. The nape of the neck is marked 'A.M.211.' The outfit is original.
Patrizia Bonato collection, Venice.

'Sultan' rag doll (page 252)

Lenci, Italy, 1925–26

32 cm (12⅝ in.)

Inspired in its design, with great attention to authentic detail in its beautifully made wooden accessories, this 'Sultan' is a superb example of the imaginative genius of the dolls made by the Lenci factory in Turin.
Patrizia Bonato collection, Venice.

Chinese rag doll (page 253, above left)

Lenci, Italy, 1925–26

30 cm ($11\frac{3}{4}$ in.)

Colour and materials have been used to great effect in the making of this delightful 'Chinaman' smoking a traditional pipe.
Patrizia Bonato collection, Venice.

Rag doll (page 253, above right)

Lenci, Italy, c. 1925

50 cm ($19\frac{1}{2}$ in.)

Pyjama-bag doll made of fabric and wearing a peasant-style costume. The slight tilt of the head and upward glance of the eyes give it considerable charm.
Patrizia Bonato collection, Venice.

Rag doll (page 253, below left)

Lenci, Italy, 1921

33 cm (13 in.)

A typical Lenci 'bambina' in perfect condition. Sewn into its dress is a ticket with the production details and patent number: 'Lenci di E. Scavini—Turin Italy—Made in Italy N. 111 N-Pat. Sept. 8, 1921—Pat, N. 142433 Bte.S.G.D.G. X 87395-Brevetto 501-178.'
Patrizia Bonato collection, Venice.

Rag doll (page 253, below right)

Lenci, Italy, 1922

40 cm ($15\frac{5}{8}$ in.)

This charming red-haired doll is a testament to the expressiveness, individuality, and high quality of the Lenci products.
Patrizia Bonato collection, Venice.

Rag doll (preceding pages)

Lenci, Italy, c. 1930

75 cm ($29\frac{1}{2}$ in.)

A fascinating doll of great character, this figure represents an adult and is dressed in a rich and elaborate regional costume.
Patrizia Bonato collection, Venice.

Rag doll

England, c. 1910

21 cm ($8\frac{3}{8}$ in.)

This doll is made of stuffed cotton printed with all the details of the doll's features, hair, and costume. The doll is stamped 'Peggie-Trade mark—Registered in all countries—Hygienic stuffing British manufacture Guaranteed.' The 'caractère' face is typical of the work of the designer Grace Gebbie Drayton, who created many famous characters for illustrated children's books as well as rag dolls, working mainly in America between 1909 and 1925. She was among the first to design dolls with round eyes, known as 'goo-goo' eyes, from which derives the generic name of 'Googlie.'
Patrizia Bonato collection, Venice.

'Little Red Riding Hood'

Dean's Rag Book Co., London,

1903–25

Stamped on cotton fabric, this doll was designed to be cut out and sewn together.
Anna Sorteni Rescigno collection, Monza.

Das Rotkäppchen.

LITTLE RED RIDING   LE PETIT CHAPERON
HOOD.   ROUGE.

DIRECTIONS.

CUT OUT THE FIGURES ROUND THE DOTTED LINES, AND PLACE THE POINTED SIDES OF THE DOLL'S FACE TO FACE, SO AS TO SEW THEM TOGETHER ON THE WRONG SIDE ROUND THE EDGES OF THE FIGURES LEAVING THE BOTTOM OPEN SO AS TO STUFF AFTERWARDS, THEN TURN INSIDE OUT. BEFORE STUFFING STITCH THROUGH THE TWO THICKNESSES ROUND THE WHITE DOTTED LINES AT THE BACK OF THE HEAD, SO THAT THE FRILL OF THE HOOD DOES NOT STUFF, BUT REMAINS FLAT. STRETCH THE BOTTOM PIECE OVER A PIECE OF THIN CARDBOARD CUT TO THE SAME SIZE BEFORE SEWING IT ON, WHICH WILL MAKE A FLAT BASE, AND ENABLE THE DOLL TO STAND. STUFF THE FIGURE, AND SEW ON THE BASE, TIE A RED RIBBON ROUND THE NECK, AND DRAW THE HOOD FORWARD, AND THE FIGURE IS COMPLETE. IF THE FRILL OF THE HOOD IS CAUGHT WITH A COUPLE OF STITCHES ON THE FRONT CLOSE TO THE HAIR, SO AS TO DRAW THE UPPER PART OF FRILL FORWARD, IT IS AN IMPROVEMENT. WOOL, BRAN, OR FLOCK MAKE THE BEST STUFFING. THE COLOURS USED ARE FAST. A CHILD CAN SUCK THEM AND DO ITSELF NO HARM. WHEN DIRTY, CAN BE PULLED TO PIECES AND WASHED.

AVIS.

DÉCOUPEZ LES DESSINS I. ET II. SUR LES LIGNES POINTILLÉES, ET PLACEZ LES CÔTÉS COLORÉS FACE À FACE, COUSEZ AINSI LE CONTOUR DES IMAGES, EN LAISSANT LE FOND OUVERT AFIN DE POUVOIR ENSUITE BOURRER LA POUPÉE, PUIS TOURNEZ L'ÉTOFFE À L'ENDROIT, AVANT DE BOURRER, COUSEZ LES DEUX PIÈCES D'ÉTOFFE EN SUIVANT LES LIGNES BLANCHES POINTILLÉES DE L'ARRIÈRE DE LA TÊTE, LAISSANT AINSI LIBRES LES FRONCES DU CHAPERON ÉTENDEZ LE DESSIN III SUR UN MORCEAU DE CARTON ASSEZ FIN, AFIN DE COMPOSER UNE BASE PLATE PERMETTANT À LA POUPÉE DE SE TENIR DEBOUT REMPLISSEZ L'INTÉRIEUR DE LAINE, DE SON, OU DE BOURRE ET COUSEZ LA BASE, SERREZ UN RUBAN ROUGE AUTOUR DU COU, TIREZ LE CHAPERON EN AVANT ET LA POUPÉE EST COMPLÈTE. ON PEUT, POUR EMBELLIR, COUDRE DE QUELQUES POINTS LE FRONCE DU CHAPERON SUR LE FRONT AFIN DE LA RAMENER UN PEU EN AVANT. LES COULEURS EMPLOYÉES SONT FORTEMENT FIXÉES. LES ENFANTS PEUVENT LES PORTER À LA BOUCHE, SANS AUCUN DANGER. QUAND LA POUPÉE SERA SALE, LA DÉCOUDRE PAR MORCEAUX AFIN DE LES LAVER SÉPARÉMENT.

D.R.G.M.   274500.

WHEN   UNE FOIS
FINISHED.   FINI.

Jerfiges Muster.

II.   I.

LONDON:
DEAN'S RAG BOOK
CO., LTD.
Manufactured in England.
PARIS: HACHETTE ET CIE.

N. 24

Boy doll in composition

France (?), 1925–30

45 cm (17⅝ in.)

Fully articulated, this doll has modelled and painted features and a skilfully made body of excellent quality. There are no trademarks to establish its precise origins.
Patrizia Bonato collection, Venice.

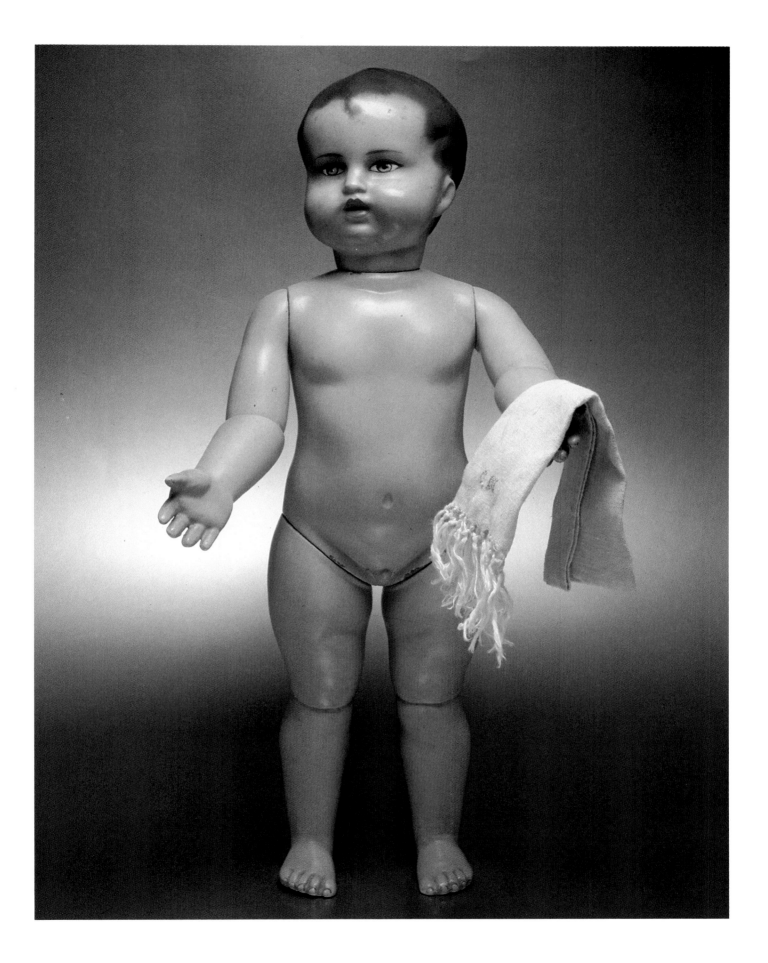

APPENDICES

25
Décembre

Joyeux Noël

COLLECTORS' NOTES

In the nineteenth century, with the pro-
liferation of toys and the shops that sold
them, many retail outlets became dolls'
hospitals, selling spare parts as well as the
dolls themselves. These 'clinics' continued
to exist until after the First World War,
when their numbers gradually declined
almost to the point of extinction. This
decline was partly a result of the evolution
of the doll, which had become less fragile
and at the same time less durable (new
models were constantly replacing outdated
ones), and partly because antique materials
were hard to find and repairs were therefore not economic. Later, as the fashion for
collecting dolls took hold, repairs became a
real problem, but in response to a new and
growing demand the few surviving dolls'
hospitals were reactivated and new ones
opened.

It is essential to be extremely cautious in
the choice of a restorer to whom to entrust
a broken antique doll, which nowadays can
fetch enormous sums. Most people engaged in the restoration of dolls carry out
this work alongside their main activity as
antique dealers and are in no way doll
specialists. The best approach is generally
to consult a real craftsman who is qualified
in this field and will be in a position to offer
sound advice. His workshop will have a
collection of spare parts, patiently gathered
together over the years and now invaluable
in the restoration of lost eyes, hands, limbs,
or internal mechanisms. He will also be
able to advise on the replacement of items
no longer available—the backcombed
nylon wig of a Fifties Barbie doll, for
example—and find alternatives that suit
the face and character of the doll in
question. Unfortunately, these experts are
few and far between.

RESTORING DOLLS

Every collector should be in a position to
judge what sort of repair is necessary to a
particular doll and whether it is possible to
carry out those repairs oneself. The following suggestions are designed to help those
who wish to do so, using as an example a
traditional doll with a bisque head in a
rather battered state.

First of all, check if the elastic—even if it
is somewhat deteriorated—is still able to
hold together the head and the various
parts of the body safely; if so, it would be a
mistake to replace it as new materials
inevitably diminish the value of the doll in
commerial as well as artistic terms. Then,
after checking the condition of the head,
one can begin the simple operation of
cleaning it. Lift the wig from the scalp and,
if necessary, remove it completely, taking
care not to damage the head in the process.
Clean off the old glue using a piece of
cotton wool soaked in warm water. The
bald head will now reveal its inner workings—and sometimes a few surprises! The
body of the doll can be cleaned with soap
and warm water in the same way, making
sure that any voice system or other mechanism in the torso does not get wet. A
toothbrush can be used to remove dust and
dirt from the joints. The inside of the head
should merely be dusted and not washed,
particularly if it contains any mechanical
parts. Great satisfaction will be derived
from seeing the colour and luminosity of
the porcelain gradually return as the grime
is removed, but the cleaning operation may
also reveal cracks and chips that were not
apparent before. There is little that can be
done about them, beyond cleaning the dirt

out of the cracks as much as possible with
soap and water; avoid using strong solvents
such as acetone (nail-polish remover), tur-
pentine, nitrates, or bleach, as they invariably leave indelible yellow rings. The most
effective method is to apply a series of
cotton wool compresses soaked in hot
water with plenty of soap; after several
applications, rub the area gently and leave
the hot compress in place until the dirt has
been washed out.

If the head has been broken and badly
repaired, remove it gently from the body
and place it in a basin of warm water. If the
glue is old it will be easy to separate the
various parts, and to remove the chalk
holding the eyes in place. Clean and dry the
edges of the broken pieces very carefully
and thoroughly before resticking them
with a strong modern glue. Then replace
the eyes, using the original chalk. Never
attempt to repaint the face of an antique
doll; the result, even in the hands of an
expert, is invariably unsatisfactory. The
only time it may be acceptable—and that
depends ultimately on personal choice—is
when a head is very badly broken and
pieces are missing. As far as commercial
value is concerned, it is always better to
have a broken and well-glued doll that
shows clearly the extent of its damage than
one that has been repainted, concealing
who knows what under layers of new
paint.

Once the head is repaired, one can turn
to the body. With traditional bodies made
of papier-mâché, composition, or wood, it
is always preferable to retain the original
materials used to link the limbs to the torso.
The paint work may be flaking, or the
entire surface of the body may have been
repainted, as often happened in the Forties

and Fifties, giving fair-skinned nineteenth-century dolls a reddish-brown tan.

The best way to prevent further flaking is simply to use a solution of polyvinyl acetate (PVA) diluted in water and paint it on with a brush around the edges of the flakes, pressing gently for a few seconds to make the fragments stick. Again, repainting or even 'replastering' with various materials, as sometimes happens, is extremely ill-advised, though there seems to be no limit to some collectors' desire to experiment. Once the polyvinyl acetate is absolutely dry, the body can be lightly waxed with furniture polish to give it back its original sheen.

In cases where the body has been completely repainted, the offending paint can sometimes be removed with a scalpel. This can be a long, slow job requiring a good deal of patience, though if the paint is sufficiently dry and thin it should peel off without too much difficulty. If not, it is far better to avoid using solvents or paint strippers, which may simply mix the colours into a sort of paste and produce cracking and blistering, and to resign oneself to the fact that the doll has a suntan.

Another cause of anxiety among many collectors is the problem of missing fingers. If the distress results in sleepless nights, new fingers can be made using papier-mâché, but it is a difficult job that requires time and care. A doll with two fingers missing is a lot better than one with claws, which is often the outcome of a botched job.

If the body is made of kid, the problems are somewhat different. Most commonly holes are worn by the internal wires and the sawdust inside gradually leaks out. These holes can be patched by gluing in place pieces of leather taken from old gloves of the same colour and texture as the kid. If the leather of the body seems dry and stiff, a neutral lubricant or oil, easily available from shops specializing in leather goods, can be applied, always sparingly.

For dolls made entirely of wax or of wax-covered composition, the best way to clean off the thick layers of dirt that can become embedded in the surface is to use a small wad of cotton covered with soft wax and rub it gently over the entire area; it will lift the dirt easily without scratching or causing discoloration. Using a clean, soft cloth, the surface should then be buffed to bring up the shine.

The next stage is the cleaning and repair of the doll's clothes. If the original outfit still remains it is vital that the doll keeps it, no matter how tattered. If the materials are not too fragile, attempts should be made to clean the outfit. If, on the other hand, the doll is naked, the problem is harder to resolve. Having established its age and provenance, the next step is to refer to books and magazines to identify the tastes and fashions in clothes at the time it was made. Then comes the difficult part: finding suitable materials to make a new outfit in the style of the period, as well as lace, ribbons and flowers to decorate it. Reproduction dresses can be very beautiful if they complement the doll and dreadful if the poor thing is swamped by yards of lace and flounces. There is a strong tendency among collectors to overdo it; charming nineteenth-century dolls are sometimes ruined by outfits made of gaudy synthetic materials.

Then comes the question of the hair. The more fastidious collectors will throw out a tattered wig with relief as soon as a doll crosses their threshold, and replace it with a cascade of blonde ringlets—always blonde—and more often than not made of synthetic hair. For them brunettes, with their hair done in some other style, do not exist. But in truth the variety of styles was endless: apart from the traditional ringlets, there were chignons and plaits, soft waves and springy curls, the hair might be worn loose or caught back, either at the nape of the neck or on top of the head with curls falling gently to the shoulders. As with clothes, it all depended on the fashion of the moment. And the colour range was as wide as it is in real life, including every shade from black to chestnut to platinum blonde. Admittedly, a great many of the most beautiful antique French dolls, that are highly prized and extremely expensive today, had wigs made of mohair or mouflon (a Mediterranean mountain sheep) rather than real hair—among them those made by Steiner, Jumeau, Bru, and Jullien. Real hair was sometimes used but only in a limited way, at certain times, and for particular models.

So the choice of a new wig, which in any case should only be resorted to if the head is entirely bald, must take into consideration all the choices available within the bounds of historical authenticity.

The serious collector should remember that an antique doll is a fragment of the past, and that only by respecting its value as a vital piece of history can one give back to it its true character and much of its original charm.

FINDING DOLLS

So many people collect dolls today that it would be hard to assess their numbers with any accuracy; the market, as a result, has almost run dry, and opportunistic dealers with very little knowledge of the subject, have profited in every sense by pushing prices up to astronomical levels. The dolls for sale on market stalls nowadays are hardly ever worth the prices asked for them, although just occasionally a real rarity will turn up, costing no more than the everyday doll next door to it, and it certainly pays to be able to recognize the difference between the two and to know the true value of each.

An alternative source is the specialist shop, where costs generally reflect international market prices and one can be fairly sure of not being swindled. And, of course, there are auctions. Hundreds of dolls come under the hammer every year at Sotheby's and Christie's alone, and the illustrated catalogues they produce will keep one up to date with trends in the market and with current prices and availability. Armed with this knowledge, and the alert, observant eye that comes from years of searching, one will be well equipped to take advantage of any bargains that do turn up. And if prices in shops and auction rooms are out of reach, don't despair. Ask friends and relations if by any chance an old doll might be lurking in their attics: one can sometimes be lucky, and there is certainly no better way to do business.

A GUIDE TO MUSEUMS

Great Britain

LONDON

Bethnal Green Museum of Childhood
   Cambridge Heath Road
   London E2

Pollock's Toy Museum
   1 Scala Street
   London W1

London Museum

Victoria & Albert Museum

British Museum

EDINBURGH

The Museum of Childhood

WARWICK

Doll Museum

WINDSOR

Windsor Castle: The Queen's Doll's
   House

United States of America

CALIFORNIA

Santa Barbara Museum of Art
   1130 State Street, Santa Barbara

CONNECTICUT

Lyman Allyn Museum
   625 Williams Street, New London

Memory Lane Doll and Toy Museum
   Old Mystic Village, Mystic

FLORIDA

Museum of Collectible Dolls
   1117 South Florida Avenue, Lakeland

GEORGIA

Museum of Antique Dolls
   505 East President Street, Savannah

ILLINOIS

University Museums
   Illinois State University, Normal

INDIANA

Children's Museum
   3000 North Meridian Street,
   Indianapolis

MASSACHUSETTS

Children's Museum
   300 Congress Street, Boston

MICHIGAN

Children's Museum
   67 East Kirby, Detroit

MISSISSIPPI

University Museums
   University of Mississippi, University

NEW YORK

Aunt Len's Doll and Toy House
   6 Hamilton Terrace, New York

Margaret Woodbury Strong Museum
   1 Manhattan Square, Rochester

Museum of the City of New York
   1220 Fifth Avenue, New York

PENNSYLVANIA

Mary Merritt Doll Museum
   Route 2, Douglassville

RHODE ISLAND

Rhode Island Historical Society
   110 Benevolent Street, Providence

SOUTH DAKOTA

Enchanted World Doll Museum
   615 North Main, Mitchell

TEXAS

Antique Doll Museum
   1721 Broadway, Galveston

France

PARIS

Musée des Arts Décoratifs

Musée de la Mode et du Costume Palais
   Galliéra

Musée Carnavalet

Musée des Arts et Traditions Populaires

POISSY

Musée du Jouet

Monaco

Musée National de Monaco: Collection
   de Galéa

West Germany

NUREMBERG

Spielzeugmuseum der Stadt Nürberg:
   Lydia Bayer Museum

Germanisches Museum:
   Nationalmuseum

MUNICH

Spielzeugmuseum im Alten Rathausturm

Stadtmuseum

BREMEN
Focke Museum

GOSLAR
Puppen Museum

NEUSTADT
Trachtenpuppenmuseum

HAMBURG
Norddeutches Landesmuseum

GREFRATH
Spielzeugmuseum Sammlung Klein:
    Niederreinischen Freilichtmuseum

East Germany

ARNSTADT
Museen der Stadt Arnstadt

SONNEBERG
Deutches Spielzeugmuseum

WALTERSHAUSEN
Heimatmuseum Schloss Tenneberg

Switzerland

BASLE
Kirchgartenmuseum

Spielzeug und Dorfmuseum:
    Wettesteinhaus

ZURICH
Wohnmuseum

Austria

SALZBURG
Museum Carolinum Augusteum
    Vocklamart-Salzkammergut
Schloss Walchen: Kinderweltmuseum

Holland

AMSTERDAM
Rijksmuseum

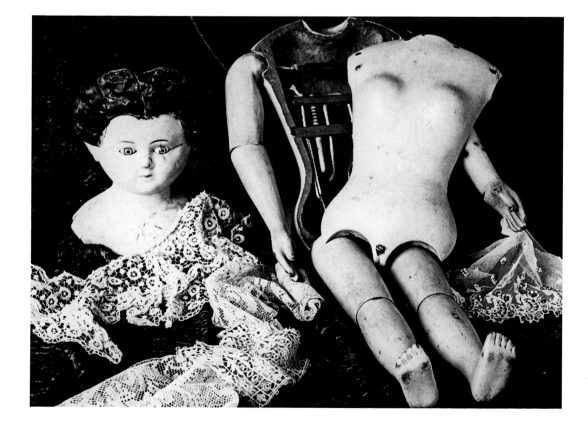

TECHNICAL DETAILS

This checklist has been compiled to help the collector make a detailed analyis of all aspects of the dolls in his or her collection. Under three headings are listed the relevant features necessary to assess the character, value and provenance of an antique doll. The page can be photocopied to serve as the basis of a catalogue of the items in a collection, or as a reference before making a purchase.

Manufacturer _____

Nationality _____

Reference Numbers _____

Approximate date of production ____

Height _____

HEAD

Materials

bisque _____

porcelain _____

Parian _____

wood _____

composition _____

wax-coated composition _____

papier-mâché _____

other _____

Trademark

die-stamp _____

etched mark _____

relief mark _____

label _____

other _____

Size

French _____

German _____

Ears

applied _____

modelled with head _____

pierced _____

unpierced _____

Neck

egg-shaped _____

flange _____

modelled with shoulders _____

articulated or fixed _____

Eyes

painted _____

French (fixed glass): colour and type
_____

German: colour and type _____

mobile glass: type of mechanism ____

Eyelashes

painted _____

applied _____

Eyebrows

painted _____

shaped _____

in relief _____

flat _____

Mouth

open _____

with or without teeth _____

tongue _____

half-open _____

closed _____

mechanism _____

Nose

modelled _____

painted _____

pierced nostrils _____

Skull

cork _____

papier-mâché _____

other _____

Hair

real hair _____

mohair _____

modelled and painted _____

Damage and repairs

manufacturing faults _____

cracks _____

missing parts _____

replastering _____

repainting _____

BODY

Trademarks _____

Labels _____

Reference Numbers _____

Colour _____

Restoration _____

Damage _____

Missing parts

Replacements _____

Materials

leather _____

wood _____

composition _____

cardboard _____

other _____

Articulation

gussets _____

ball-joints _____

semi-articulated _____

fully articulated _____

caractère type _____

French type _____

German type _____

Number of pieces

limbs in bisque _____

limbs in composition _____

limbs in other materials _____

Mechanisms

new cords _____

original cords _____

elastic _____

springs _____

bellows _____

walking mechanism _____

voice mechanism _____

other _____

CLOTHES

Labels

original _____

partly original _____

contemporary with doll _____

reproduction _____

modern _____

Shoes

Accessories

BIBLIOGRAPHY

Bayer, L., *Das Spilzeug Museum der Stadt.* Nuremberg, 1979.

Brechtu, U., *Kostbare Puppen.* Frankfurt, 1978.

Caillois, R., *I giochi e gli uomini.* Milan, 1981.

Capia, R., *Les poupées françaises.* Paris, 1979.

Cieslik, M.J., *Europaische puppen.* Munich, 1979.

Coleman, D.S., E.A. and E.J., *The Collector's Encyclopedia of Dolls*, vol. I. New York, 1968; London, 1970. *The Collector's Encyclopedia of Dolls*, vol. II. London and New York, 1986. *The Collector's Book of Dolls Clothes.* London, 1976.

Coleman, D.S., *Lenci Dolls.* United States, 1977.

Desmonde, K., *Dolls.* London, 1974.

Foulke, J., *Gebrüder Heubach Dolls.* United States, 1980.

Fox, C., *The Doll.* New York, 1972.

Fraser, A., *Dolls.* New York, 1963.

Lavitt, W., *The Knopf Collectors' Guides to American Antiques: Dolls.* New York, 1983.

Noble, J., *Beautiful Dolls.* New York, 1978.

Perrot, P., *Il sopra e il sotto della borghesia.* Milan, 1982.

Rauccio Brovarone, A., *Pupeide.* Turin, 1973.

Remise, J., and Fondin, J., *The Golden Age of Toys.* Lausanne, 1967.

Ricci, F.M., *Androide.* Milan, 1980.

Richter, L., *Franzosische Puppen.* Munich, 1981. *Puppenstars.* Munich, 1984.

Smith, P.R., *Kestner and Simon & Halbig Dolls, 1804–1930.* United States, 1976. *French Dolls.* United States, 1979. *China and Parian Dolls.* United States, 1980.

Stablein, R., *Altes Holzspielzeug aus Groden.* Dortmund, 1981.

Theimer, F., *Histoire et étude de la S.F.B.J.* Paris, 1985. *Le Bébé Jumeau.* Paris, 1985. *Une Histoire 'Parisienne' Leopold et Calixte Huret.* Paris, 1986.

Weisse, E., and Stauffacher, R., *Automates et instruments de musique mécaniques.* Frieburg, 1976.

White, G., *European and American Dolls.* London, 1966.

Whitton, M., *The Jumeau Doll.* New York, 1980.

CATALOGUES

Ehret, G., Fischer, M., and Zweig, V.G., *Puppen.* Munich, 1980.

Theimer, F., *Repertoire des marques et cote des poupées françaises.* Paris, 1985.

Wegner, G., *Puppen.* Julich Koslar, Germany, 1985.

Annual of the magazine *Polichinelle.* Paris, 1985–86.

Balocchi, giochi, giocattoli e modellismo. Trieste, 1985.

Catalogues of Sotheby's auctions. London, 1984, 1985, 1986.

Come giocavamo. Milan, 1984.

Crepereia Tryphaena. Milan and Venice, 1983.

Il paese dei balocchi. Colorno, 1983.

Il trascorso presente, bambole giocattoli automi, 1830–1930. Venice, 1982.

La mode et les poupées. Paris, 1982.

Per una bambola. Canneto sull'Oglio, Mantua, 1984.

Poupée jouet, poupée reflets. Paris, 1982.

ACKNOWLEDGMENTS

The publishers would like to thank the following for their kind help and cooperation:

Princess Bona Borromeo, for making available the dolls in the Borromeo collection, Isola Madre, Italy.

Patrizia Bonato, for the loan of photographic material and for allowing the dolls in her collection to be photographed.

Elio Filoni, Marika Rossi, Mario Guadagnino, Vittorio Colombo, and Anna Sorteni Rescigno for having kindly made it possible to photograph the dolls in their collections.

Patrizia Martini for the loan of contemporary postcards published here.

Luisa Ronchini for the use of the previously unpublished Lenci catalogue cover.

Doretta Davanzo Poli for her invaluable help in researching the documents of the period.

Eliana Martinalli for the loan of the photograph of the 'Jumeau triste' in her possession.

The Craftsman's Studio of Santa Guistina in Venice for the restoration of some of the dolls photographed here.

Mattell for providing and allowing the reproduction of the photographs of the Barbie doll that appear on page 81.

The author would like particularly to thank all those who have offered him patient and affectionate support throughout his research on this project, and who have provided invaluable ideas and advice.

PICTURE SOURCES

Page 9; Archives photographiques, Paris (Foto Nadar): pages 11, 13; Musei Capitolini, Antiquarium Communale, Rome (Foto Araldo De Luca): page 12; British Museum, London: pages 14, 21, 23; Max von Boehn, *Puppen und Puppenspiele*, Munich, 1929: page 17; Kunsthistorishes Museum, Vienna (Foto Meyer): page 16; Victoria and Albert Museum, London: pages 18, 22; *Il bazar-giornale illustrato delle famiglie*, August 1870 (page 18) and October 1871 (page 22): page 27; Borromeo collection, Isola Madre, Italy: page 38; Alison Adburgham, *Shopping in Style*, London, 1979: page 39; Patrizia Bonato collection, Venice: page 40; *An Old-fashioned Christmas in Illustration and Decoration*, New York, 1970: pages 42, 44, 45, 79; Margaret Whitton, *The Jumeau Doll*, New York, 1980: page 48; *Children of the Past in Photographic Portraits*, New York, 1978: page 51; *Petite Echo de la Mode*, December 1892: page 69; Enrico Castruccio archive, Milan: page 75; Rosita Levi Pisetzky, *Storia del Costume in Italia*, vol. V, Milan, 1969.